INTERMEDIATE MODERN

2

SOCIAL ISSUES IN THE UK

JOHN McTAGGART
and ALLAN GRIEVE

Hodder Gibson
2A Christie Street, Paisley, PA1 1NB

CONTENTS

INTRODUCTION

S*ocial Issues in the UK* has been written to meet the needs of students taking Intermediate 1 and Intermediate 2 courses in Higher Modern Studies. It can be used in association with support materials published by the Higher Still Development Unit and also by BBC Scotland Education.

The book aims to provide students with the necessary knowledge and understanding to succeed at either Intermediate 1 or Intermediate 2 level. There are also activities which seek to develop the evaluating skills required by the course. Activities have been set to challenge pupils at Intermediate 1 and Intermediate 2 levels. We believe that the classroom teacher is best placed to know which activities are most appropriate for individual pupils.

The use of extended writing activities is also included to enable students to succeed at Intermediate 2 level, and also to prepare them for progression to Higher Modern Studies. 'Hamburger essays' are more appropriate, but not exclusively, for Intermediate 2 pupils.

THE HAMBURGER ESSAY

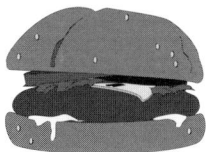

This is an attempt to develop students' skills in extended writing. Students should use the hamburger method to answer a specific question in detail, giving examples. The teacher may wish to add a mark, we recommend out of ten, to grade the work.

◆ *Part One: Introduction (the bread on the top)*
State clearly what the issue is and what your conclusion shall be. It may explain any 'big words' that will be used.

◆ *Part Two: Main part (the meat in the middle)*
Give several reasons for your answer. This should look at different points of view and should not be biased. It should give examples to show understanding.

◆ *Part Three: Conclusion (the bread on the bottom)*
This should sum up your findings, giving your recommendations where appropriate. The conclusion should always consider how your recommendations are to be paid for.

Reference will be made to BBC Scotland audio and video tapes *Crime and the Law* (April 2001) and *Gender and Race* (1999) which have been made for Intermediate 1 and 2. These references are made to help students write detailed investigations on key social issues.

Students are encouraged to develop independent learning through social research and the use of ICT. A number of useful websites are highlighted.

Modern Studies texts have always struck the balance between coverage of UK and specifically Scottish issues. Given the relevant powers that have been devolved to the Scottish parliament, there is a greater Scottish dimension in this text, especially in Chapters Two and Three.

Students are also encouraged to debate and discuss social issues in an organised, responsible way. A series of topical (and hopefully enjoyable) debates are highlighted for potential student use. The following rules of engagement can be used to help pupils prepare for the debates. It goes without saying that teachers can adapt these rules to suit their own circumstances.

RULES OF ENGAGEMENT

Speaking for the motion

Prepare a case which has three main points. This is your chance to set the agenda. The opposition have to reply to your arguments. Use the textbook, support materials and your own knowledge to prepare your case. Humour is always a good idea. Your aim is to convince the audience that your arguments are right.

Structure

Your speech should have a clear introduction, middle and conclusion. In your introduction, spell out what you are going to say; in the middle say it; and in your conclusion, remind everyone of what you have just said.

In a Modern Studies speech, it is important to recommend that certain things should or should not be done. You must, however, explain how these things are possible and how they can be paid for.

Opposing the speech

It is your job to destroy the arguments presented by the proposition. You should not be personal about it – it is the arguments you oppose, not the person. Your job is slightly more difficult than the proposition, because you must *respond* to the arguments that he/she presents. You cannot predict what they are likely to say, but you should be able to *anticipate* the key arguments that are presented.

Prepare classic counter arguments that are appealing to those who are listening. Your speech should follow the same structure as the proposition. Your speech will be more convincing if you can provide social and economic evidence against the proposition's views.

1

GENDER AND RACE

This chapter will look at different aspects of **Gender and Racial Equality**. It is divided into two parts; Part One will look at gender issues and Part Two racial issues. Part One will:
- ◆ examine why gender stereotypes are becoming increasingly out of date
- ◆ discuss the effectiveness of laws which try to prevent gender discrimination
- ◆ explain the difference between direct and indirect gender discrimination
- ◆ analyse how gender can affect career opportunities
- ◆ examine the relationship between a person's gender and their health
- ◆ examine the differences in political representation between men and women

Part Two will:
- ◆ examine the origins of racial prejudice
- ◆ examine the effectiveness of laws which try to prevent racial discrimination
- ◆ describe the different types of racism; direct, indirect and institutional
- ◆ analyse how race can affect career opportunities
- ◆ examine the issues surrounding race and the criminal justice system
- ◆ examine the differences in political representation between Britain's different racial groups

SEXIST STEREOTYPES

Sexist stereotypes run deep in our society. They are based on the historical dominance that men had over women. Ideas that men were the stronger, more capable sex were used to keep women 'in their place', which was usually at home or in the kitchen. Women have always resisted this dominance. The Suffragettes eventually won women the right to vote in the UK in 1928 after protests that included hunger strikes and suicide. The women's movement of the 1960s put pressure on government to change laws to ensure that women would be treated equally at school and at work. Stereotypes can cause damage when they lead to prejudice and, ultimately, discrimination.

A stereotype is something we believe all people of a certain group to be like. It is closely linked to prejudice. Prejudice means to pre-judge people without having met them. For example, stereotypes of

Scots often suggest meanness, drunkenness or violence. Because stereotypes are often negative, this can lead to prejudiced views. Women and ethnic minorities are two groups of people whose lives are strongly affected by negative stereotyping.

It would be wrong to deny that *some* gender stereotypes are not based on fact. Many women do have different interests than men. To test this hypothesis, try to bring into the classroom some examples of 'lifestyle' magazines, such as the women's magazine *Red* or men's magazine *FHM*.

ACTIVITY

Draw up a table and match the following stereotype to the gender you feel it most accurately belongs to.

Cares about clothes – Hard working at school – Good at sports – Strong – Good with young children – Good at fixing cars – Bad drivers – Likes football – Can handle pressure – Cries when upset – Talks a lot on the telephone – Drinks beer – Enjoys shopping – Reliable – Cares about figure – Cares about diet – Spends money on toiletries.

ACTIVITY

Complete the following table for other magazines you know of

Magazine	Male/female/both	Reasons

Few people would seriously argue that all men are the same as all women. The writers of the above magazines know exactly the type of people who are likely to read their magazine. Market research will show not just the gender, but the age group, ethnic background and income of its readers. The advertising inside the magazine will reflect this. The reality is that most men and women do have different characteristics and traits. However, stereotypes can never be used as evidence of social/economic reality. Stereotypes may give us a broad idea of what a man or woman may like, but this can never be assumed to be completely accurate for *all* people.

ACTIVITIES

1 *"Stereotypes are just harmless fun."*
   "Stereotypes can be damaging."
   Which point of view do you agree with most? Give reasons for your answer.
2 For three popular magazines that you know, describe the 'target audience' in terms of age, gender and income group.

OUTDATED STEREOTYPES

Society has changed so quickly in recent years that many former all-male or all-female traits are now relevant to both sexes. For example, the high street chain store *Boots* has opened a special men's store in Edinburgh to cater for the huge increase in demand for men's toiletries. In 1999 British men spent £23.6 million on hair care. The £7.1 million spent on hair dye is more than double the figure for 1995. Opened by Gavin Hastings in 1999, the *Boots* store aims to build on the increasing demand by men for beauty products such as deodorants, aftershaves, moisturisers and other skin products. The shop, which opens at 7.30 am, also offers wet shaving, manicures and shampooing. Inside, it attempts to cultivate a more 'male' atmosphere with a chrome, steel and metal interior. The traditional *Boots* white and blue carrier bag has been replaced with a more 'macho' black and grey bag. Although women are welcome, the shop is clearly targeted at the growing male market for beauty products. Research shows that British males are among the vainest in Europe.

Boots for Men, Princess Street, Edinburgh

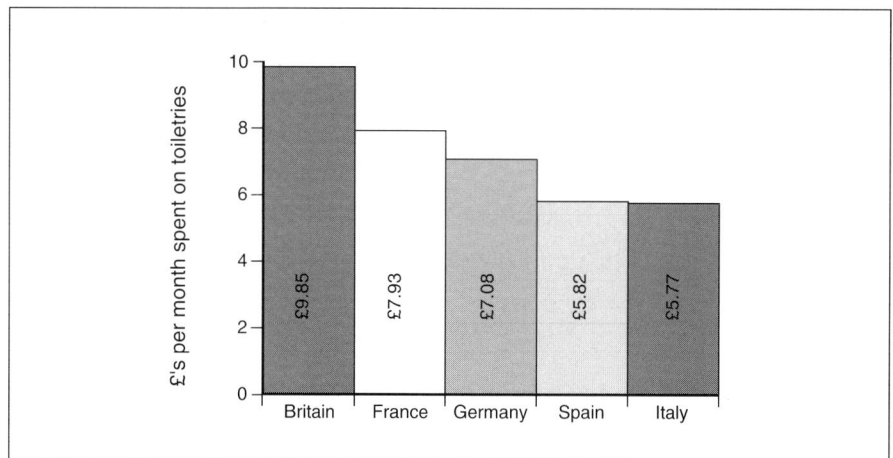

Male spending on toiletries per month, 1999

Scotland rugby hero Gavin Hastings opened the Boots for men store in Edinburgh in 1999

Weblink: www.datamonitor.com

According to one analyst, the vanity barriers for males have broken down because it is now as important for men to look good at work as it is for women. Another explained the trend on the decline in the taboo regarding men smelling and looking good.

In a similar manner, men are now buying lifestyle magazines in the same numbers as women. Newsagents sell as many men's magazines, such as *FHM* or *Loaded*, as women's magazines, like *Just Seventeen* or *Cosmopolitan*. The monthly *FHM* magazine sells 700 000 copies. The editor of *FHM*, Anthony Noguera, explains its success: *"We've led on male grooming features since day one. Everybody said it was just a poof's game, but that's rubbish"*.

As for motoring – that stereotypical male hobby – the sexist stereotype of women drivers is that they are not very good. The reality is that young males cause the majority of road accidents. Accordingly, insurance premiums for women are less than for men.

ACTIVITIES

1   Why do you think *Boots* chose Gavin Hastings to open its new men's beauty store?
2   Carry out a survey of males in your school on shopping in men's beauty stores. Your hypothesis (statement) is *"Most males would shop at a men's beauty store"*. Your task is to find out if this statement is true.

    Try for a sample of around 50. Select three key questions that will allow you to answer your hypothesis. Make a careful note of where and when the interviews took place. Present your results in bar/pie charts and analyse your findings e.g. are your results reliable? Why? Why not?

More and more men are buying magazines like FHM

Sexist stereotypes exclude one sex from opportunities in life and are based on prejudice, not fact. Sexist attitudes also do not take into account the changes that are taking place in society. Among the younger generation, at least, we are becoming much more liberal about gender equality. According to the 1998 British and European Social Attitudes Survey, only 1 in 4 people in Britain believe that it is "a man's job to earn money and a woman's job to look after the family and the home". 50% of people interviewed believe that family life does not suffer when a woman has a full-time job. 64% believed that a couple living together outside of marriage was acceptable.

GENDER DISCRIMINATION

To discriminate means to 'pick out for special treatment'. The word is usually used in a negative context, when people are unfairly treated. It is illegal today to discriminate against someone on the basis of gender or race but this does not mean that discrimination does not happen. In this section we shall look at how gender affects an individual's social and economic standard of living.

LEGISLATION ON GENDER EQUALITY

Under the Equal Pay Act 1970, women are entitled to equal pay with men when doing the same work. The Sex Discrimination Acts of 1975 and 1986 have made it illegal to treat anyone, on the grounds of sex, less favourably than a person of the opposite sex. The two Acts aim to help create real equality of opportunity for males and females. Men are also entitled to use the laws if they feel unfairly treated. The main weakness of the legislation, however, is that discrimination can be hard to prove. A person may feel they have been the victim of sex discrimination, but proving it can be difficult, and expensive. Sex discrimination is not allowed in employment, education, the provision of housing, goods, facilities and services, and advertising. These are discussed in more detail below.

Employment
Employers cannot describe jobs as being 'for men' or 'for women', except in certain limited circumstances such as counselling jobs where a person of a specific sex would be most appropriate. This also applies to promotion or training. Opportunities must be equally open to both sexes. It is good practice for a company to have an equal opportunities policy. This means that a company will be aware that discrimination is possible, unless actively discouraged. An employer will also take steps to ensure that both sexes have equal chances of promotion in the company. It is unlawful to discriminate because a person is married or unmarried.

FACTFILE

1977 First woman fire-fighter: Mary Langdon
1983 First woman train driver: Anne Winter
1987 First male midwife, Robin Bowyer, begins his training
1995 First woman Chief Constable: Pauline Clare, Lancashire Constabulary
1995 First woman qualified motor mechanic in Scotland: Kirsty Aitken

Education

There must be equal opportunities in schools. The Careers Service must not discriminate in the advice it offers, and courses such as CDT or Home Economics, which in the past have been dominated by one sex, must be open to all. Single-sex schools are still allowed, but all subjects should be offered.

The provision of housing, goods, facilities and services

In housing, a house should not be refused on the basis of gender. Similarly, a hotel or restaurant may not refuse you accommodation or refreshment on the basis of your sex. In financial services, banks and building societies cannot refuse credit on the basis of gender.

Advertising

If you feel that an advertisement discriminates against you on the basis of sex, you have the right to complain to the Advertising Standards Authority.

THE EQUAL OPPORTUNITIES COMMISSION (EOC)

The EOC was set up in 1975 to try to make sure that the Equal Pay Act and the Sex Discrimination Act were put into practice. It provides a number of services for individuals and employers. In the first place, it tries to ensure that discrimination does not occur, by educating about the rights and responsibilities that people have under the law. It can make representation to government suggesting changes in the law, and will offer advice to people if they feel they have been discriminated against. The EOC has the right to investigate areas of inequality and, if it wishes, provide legal help for individuals challenging sex discrimination.

The EOC is there to end sex discrimination against men as well as women. It used to be the law that women were entitled to a state pension and free prescriptions at the age of 60, but men had to wait until 65. The EOC campaigned against this inequality. Since 1995, elderly males can now get free prescriptions at the same age as women and the pension age will be 65 for both sexes by 2020.

ACTIVITIES

1 What laws are there to create equal opportunities for men and women?
2 Describe the main aims of these laws.
3 What weaknesses are there in the laws?
4 Describe the three things that the Equal Opportunities Commission (EOC) can do to help achieve equal opportunities.
5 *"The EOC helps men as well as women".* What evidence is there to support this statement?

DIRECT AND INDIRECT DISCRIMINATION

There are two types of discrimination. The first is direct discrimination. This is the most obvious and is the easiest to prove. For example, if an employer sacks a woman for having a baby, this is direct discrimination and is illegal.

Fish fryer who was groped and fired gets £5457

A fish fryer who claimed a colleague called her a "slapper" and groped her breasts won her sex discrimination claim and £5457 in compensation. An industrial tribunal today heard how Ms X, 20, enjoyed working at a fish and chip shop in Dundee until a friend of the owners, Mr Y, started working alongside her. She was frequently upset at the way he verbally harassed her. Matters came to a head one night when she claimed Mr Y fondled her breasts and rubbed her back. Ms X tried, unsuccessfully, to get a colleague to cover for her and phoned her mother to tell her about the incident.

She continued to work at the fish and chip shop but kept away from Mr Y. She said he continued following her around. She claimed that she complained to the boss, Mr Z, but that he refused to take the matter further. Ms X told the tribunal that Mr Z refused to listen to a witness and warned her not to go to the police. He called her a liar and sacked her from her £125 a week job when she insisted she wasn't. Ms X reported the matter to the police, but Mr Y had left the country and the police could not proceed with the enquiry.

The tribunal said it had no difficulty believing the evidence of Ms X. It noted that Ms X had been extremely distressed by the verbal and physical harassment. This was made worse by Mr Z's refusal to investigate her genuine complaints and his subsequent sacking of her. She managed to get another job as a cleaner but was earning only £52 a week.

Adapted from The Herald, *27 January 1999*

Indirect discrimination is less obvious, and much more difficult to define. It means that conditions at work, for example in recruiting or promoting workers, are open to all, but are much easier for one sex than the other. If, for example, an employer made it a condition for promotion that overtime had to be done in the evenings when a woman has a child care role, this could be indirect discrimination.

If a man or a woman feels they have been discriminated against on the basis of gender, he/she has the right to take a complaint to the County Court in England or Wales, or the Sheriff Court in Scotland. He/she may go to the EOC for advice. If the EOC believes the individual has a case, legal help may be available.

CONTINUED INEQUALITIES

Despite acts of Parliament and the EOC, there is a great deal of evidence to show that women, in general, still do not have the same opportunities as men. It appears that changing the law is only the first step. To achieve genuine gender equality will take not only political change, but also changes in social attitudes and roles in child care and housework.

More than 20 years after the first Sex Discrimination Act, women still earn less than men and do more low skilled and low status jobs. The following tables show the differences between men and women at work.

	1977	1997
men	177	903
women	127	723

Table 1 Hourly earnings (pence per hour) (Source: EOC, 1998)

	Men	Women
managers and administrators	204 000	105 000
clerical and secretarial	88 000	244 000
sales and checkout assistants	30 000	115 000

Table 2 Employment by occupation, 1997 (Source: EOC, 1998)

	Men	Women
all grades	48.2%	51.8%
headteachers	90.3%	9.7%
deputy headteachers	81.7%	18.3%
assistant headteachers	68.8%	31.2%
principal teachers	61.6%	38.4%
unpromoted teachers	36.3%	63.7%

Table 3 Publicly funded secondary schools in Scotland, 1997 (Source: Scottish Office Education Department, 1998)

INVESTIGATION

Your title is "Equality at Work?"

Your possible resources are:
◆ Social Issues in the UK textbook
◆ EOC website www.eoc.org.uk
◆ BBC Scotland video Gender and Race: Employment
◆ BBC Scotland audio tape Gender and Race

On four separate pages, work through the following:

1 Explain how the law tries to achieve Equal Opportunities at work.
2 Explain direct discrimination, giving examples.
3 Explain indirect discrimination, giving examples.
4 Explain what is meant by the 'glass ceiling', giving examples.

You should have a closing page (conclusion) which sums up whether men and women have equal opportunities at work.

ACTIVITIES

1 "Women have nothing to moan about any more. Women have achieved equality to men." Statement by Mark Bailey.
   Using evidence from Tables 1, 2 and 3, give three reasons why Mark Bailey could be accused of being selective in his use of facts.
2 Give an example of direct sex discrimination from The Herald newspaper article.
3 Do you feel that the Sex Discrimination Act was effective in this case? Give reasons for your answer.

Fiona Nicholson is the head of a team of lawyers at the top Scottish law firm Maclay Murray and Spens

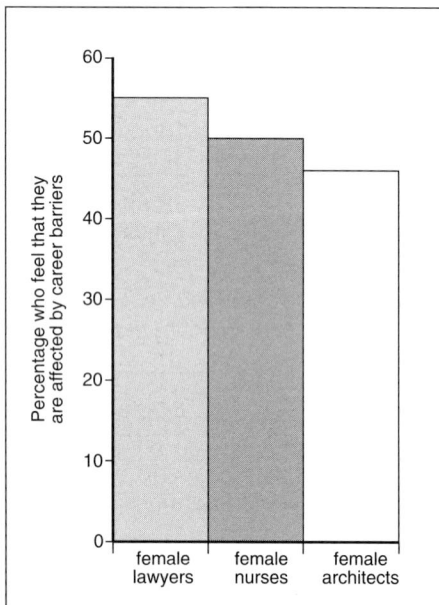

Do you feel affected by career barriers?

THE 'GLASS CEILING'

The 'glass ceiling' is a term used when women are employed in an organisation, but not in positions of high responsibility. This means that women can see that the top jobs are available, but there are social and economic barriers that prevent them winning those jobs. Some women have broken the glass ceiling. For example, Margaret Thatcher became the first female Prime Minister in 1979 and Fiona Nicholson (left) is head of a team of lawyers at the top Scottish law firm of Maclay Murray & Spens.

However, there is much evidence to suggest that the glass ceiling continues to exist. A study by researchers at Dundee University in 1999 showed that women continue to face barriers to their career prospects. The study looked at the working lives of professional men and women over a two year period. While direct discrimination was not so obvious, professional women *were* disadvantaged. More than half of the women surveyed said that promotion structures favoured men. 43% of women felt a glass ceiling existed in their profession. 35% of men agreed.

REASONS FOR CAREER BARRIERS

The first reason given in the study was the 'long hours culture' of many professions. UK workers are particularly affected by the attitude that those who spend long hours at work deserve promotion more than those who do not. As women are more likely than men to have domestic responsibilities, men can tend to stay later at work and socialise ('rub shoulders with the boss') after working hours. The study found that in professions such as dentistry, where women could work more flexibly on a part-time basis, there were fewer barriers to promotion.

The second reason given was the maternity leave that women took. This enabled their male colleagues to gain experience and training which women never caught up with. In 2000 the Labour Government introduced paternity leave, which allows men to take the same time off as women to look after newly-born children. It is hoped that this will lead to more men looking after children.

CASE STUDY

Primary teaching in Scotland

In the world of primary teaching, gender stereotyping meets discrimination. 90.8% of Scottish primary teachers are female (1996 figures). Less than 10% are male. Despite this, of the small number who are male, 27.3% have become headteachers. This can be contrasted with the picture in secondary schools. Here, 51.8% are female, yet only 9.7% are headteachers. There are no legal barriers to women becoming headteachers. In fact, in primary teaching, women outnumber men by a ratio of 9 to 1. In secondary teaching, there are slightly more women than men. Yet it is men who hold the top jobs. Education is a classic example of the glass ceiling.

Alan Richards, a primary teacher in Stranraer, explains:

"If you have a stereotypical male view of what a career is about, primary teaching won't appeal. Teaching at this level is about working with others rather than working above them, a different perspective to that of most males, who still look at a career in terms of how far they can go, and what they have to do to get there. Men tend to want to be in control – so you get a low percentage of men in primary schools but a high proportion of them are in the management sector."

Paul Deponio is head teacher at an Edinburgh primary school. There are only six male teachers out of a total of 20 teaching staff. Paul also has a male deputy head.

"The disincentive to men lies in the age of the children – they see it all as wiping noses and bottoms, although I must say I have never done that in 26 years of teaching primary children."

Scotland on Sunday 25/9/96

Read the profiles of these two Scottish primary teachers:

	Alasdair	Diane
Age	27	27
Occupation	Primary Assistant Head Teacher	Primary Teacher
Salary	£28,000	£20,000
Marital status	Married, one child	Married, two children
Career plans	Studying for the Scottish Head Teacher qualification. Hopes to be a head within five years	Just returned to work after having second child. Would like promotion, but family life comes first.
Hobbies	Five-a-side football, golf	Reading

ACTIVITIES

1 What evidence is there that men and women feel there is not equality at work?

2 Describe what is meant by the 'glass ceiling'.

3 Explain the reasons why, despite equal opportunities laws, the glass ceiling exists.

There are at least three possible explanations for the glass ceiling in primary education. The first explanation is good old fashioned prejudice. Some women, because of years of socialisation, actually believe that men are in fact more suited to positions of leadership. Some women believe it is 'unnatural' for a woman to be boss instead of Alasdair, and will make way for him.

A second reason is Diane's role as child rearer and organiser of domestic life at home. While Alasdair has time to prepare for his management course, Diane is changing nappies and making dinner.

By the time she has returned from her career break, Alasdair has become Assistant Headteacher, and is well on the way to becoming a Headteacher.

A third reason is the motivation that Alasdair will possess. Perhaps the only male in the staffroom, he will be the butt of female banter. Excluded from the female bonding, he will be more comfortable as a 'Chief' rather than an 'Indian'. His other primary male colleagues will be in positions of management. His friends outside of teaching (who think primary teaching is a 'cissy job' anyway) will be climbing the promotion ladder. He will feel strong peer group pressure to make it to the top to show his masculine credentials. Diane, on the other hand, may not possess this motivation. On the contrary, her energies are taken up looking after two young children. Promotion would be nice, but her CV is not nearly as impressive as Alasdair's.

ACTIVITIES

1 Describe how Alasdair has a more comfortable standard of living than Diane.
2 Explain why the glass ceiling may prevent Diane, but not Alasdair, becoming a Primary Headteacher.

The inequalities between men and women are all the more stark when we consider that girls are doing much better than boys at school.

WHY DO BOYS FAIL AT SCHOOL?

Boys' lack of success at school has become a concern for the government. Several reasons have been put forward for the continuing dominance of girls over boys at school.

Peer group pressure

Among boys, doing well at school is not valued. Attributes such as toughness, being good at football and 'being hard' are valued more. However, activities which foster 'hardness', such as disrupting classes, bunking off or fighting, are not those that

% gaining 1–4 Higher Grades	Boys	Girls
1975	28	30
1985	31	37
1995	38	47

% gaining 5 Higher Grades	Boys	Girls
1975	10	8
1985	12	12
1995	16	20

% gaining no awards at school	Boys	Girls
1975	38	35
1985	25	22
1995	10	8

Comparing boys' and girls' school performance (Source: SQA, 1997)

"Girls are doing much better than boys at school. In fact, the gap between girls and boys is widening all the time." Statement by Colleen McGlade.

1 To what extent does the evidence support the viewpoint of Colleen McGlade?
2 Give reasons why boys are doing less well at school than girls.
3 For each reason, describe from your experiences at school whether these explanations are valid.
4 What do you think could be done to improve boys' performance at school?

ACTIVITIES

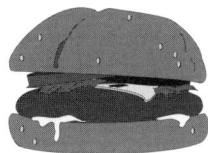

Extended Writing
Sum up the reasons why gender inequalities continue in the UK.

lead to educational success. By contrast, the girls' peer group values doing well at school. Listening in class, doing work without supervision and completing homework are the activities that lead to exam success.

Lack of role models

It is argued that boys do not come into contact with enough males in teaching, especially at primary school. This, it is claimed, leads to a lack of good work habits being instilled at an early age. School is therefore seen as a 'girls' thing', not a place where male success is rewarded. It can, of course, be argued that girls simply mature quicker than boys do and realise at a much earlier age the importance of education.

WHY DOES DISCRIMINATION CONTINUE?

The existence of negative gender stereotypes is one reason. Another is that indirect discrimination can be very difficult to prove. A man or woman may feel that gender was an issue during a job interview, but find it hard to prove. Breaking down the glass ceiling at work requires changes to the roles men and women play in society at large.

Child care

It is still the case that women, overwhelmingly, take responsibility for looking after children. When women take time off work to raise children, their male contemporaries are gaining work experience and training to climb the career ladder. Hence, when a woman goes back to work, after a 'career gap', male employees, such as Alasdair, have a better CV when applying for jobs.

The division of labour within the family

While more women are going out to work and many 'traditional' attitudes have changed, it is still mostly women who do the bulk of time-consuming household chores. Research for the British and European Social Attitudes survey shows that in 1998, eight out of 10 women did the washing and ironing, as well as caring for the sick. The only difference was in households where the woman earned more than the man, but even here, women did the laundry in 63% of these households.

SPORT: THE BARRIERS COME DOWN

Perhaps the most vivid example of outdated stereotypes lies in football. The 'beautiful game' used to be an overwhelmingly male sport. Until recently, few football grounds had facilities for female fans, few girls played football and women's football was a minority interest. By contrast, the 1999 FIFA Women's World Cup Final saw the USA defeat China in front of a sell out 90 000 crowd.

Women's FIFA Football World Cup Final, 1999

Today, female football fans are commonplace. The move to all-seater stadia has helped to create a more civilised atmosphere inside football grounds. Gangs of males can no longer form an intimidating mob quite so easily. Top football clubs have improved toilet and catering facilities as they see the benefits of attracting female custom. According to one teenage football fan *"I prefer going to football than pop concerts. Boyzone will be all over in a year or two. I can follow Manchester United forever."*

ACTIVITIES

1 Give three reasons why more women are now attending football games.
2 Carry out a survey of female attendance at football games. Your hypothesis is "Teenage girls today prefer going to a football match than a pop concert". Your task is to find out if this statement is true.
  Select three key questions that will enable you to answer your hypothesis.
  Make a careful note of where and when the interviews took place.
  Present your findings on a bar chart or pie chart. Analyse your results.

"Who's the female in the black?"

In 1999, a French 'assistant referee' (*not* a lines*man*!), Nely Viennot, played a crucial part in the sending off of Scotland defender Matt Elliot in the Euro 2000 qualifying game against the Faroe Islands. Today, in Scotland, there are around 44 female referees. This compares with over 2200 male referees.

Bank services manager Fiona Edwards has a Grade 3 Referee Qualification and hopes to achieve Grade 1 status. This would allow her to referee top Premier League, European and international matches.

According to George Cummings, SFA Development Director, *"as far as refs are concerned the future is female"*.

Stirling Golf Club

Private organisations are exempt from the Sex Discrimination Act. If a group of men or women form a club and they pay for it with their own money, it is entirely their private business who they allow to be a member. If however it benefits from a government service, like refuse collection, it must not discriminate.

Stirling Golf Club is one of Scotland's oldest and most prestigious clubs. Until 1998, it did not allow women access to the same facilities as men. For example, the club TV was kept in the men's lounge. Like many organisations, Stirling Golf Club is entitled to apply for National Lottery grants to improve facilities. However, a condition of receiving lottery cash is that facilities must be open to all. At its 1998 Annual General Meeting, the mostly male members voted against receiving a £24,000 grant from the National Lottery to improve and extend its clubhouse. One of the conditions of receiving the grant was that women should have equal access to the clubhouse. This decision was reversed when the club appointed a new captain who campaigned to overturn the decision. Stirling Golf Club now has equal opportunities for men and women.

ACTIVITIES

1 What evidence is there for and against the views of George Cummings on female referees?
2 Why do you think private associations are exempt from some aspects of the Sex Discrimination Act?
3 Why do you think the National Lottery insists on equal opportunities before awarding grants to private associations?

Inequalities in health

In general, women can expect to live longer than men. Average life expectancy for women in the UK has reached 79, while the average man can expect to live until 73. On the other hand, women are more likely to suffer from illness and poorer health throughout their life than men. In 1996–1997, women in nearly all age groups were more likely than men to have health problems.

The most common cause of death for women below the age of 65 is now breast cancer. Overall, one in 10 women will develop it at some point in their life. The good news is that survival rates are significantly increased if the disease is traced early on. Thanks to government health campaigns, the present generation of young women are much better informed about being screened for breast cancer. Cervical cancer is another major cause of death. Like breast cancer, it is not the killer it once was if it is diagnosed at an early stage.

Coronary heart disease remains a major cause of death for both sexes, but it is much more serious for men. Men, in general, tend to

Self-reported health problems: by gender and age, 1996–97

United Kingdom					Percentages
	16–44	45–64	65–74	75 and over	All aged 16 and over
Males					
Pain or discomfort	18	39	52	56	32
Mobility	6	22	36	50	18
Anxiety or depression	12	19	20	19	15
Problems performing usual activities	5	16	21	27	12
Problems with self-care	1	6	8	14	5
Females					
Pain or discomfort	20	40	51	65	34
Mobility	6	21	37	60	19
Anxiety or depression	18	24	25	30	22
Problems performing usual activities	7	17	23	40	15
Problems with self-care	2	5	9	21	6

Source: General Household Survey, Office for National Statistics; Continuous Household Survey, Northern Ireland Statistics and Research Agency

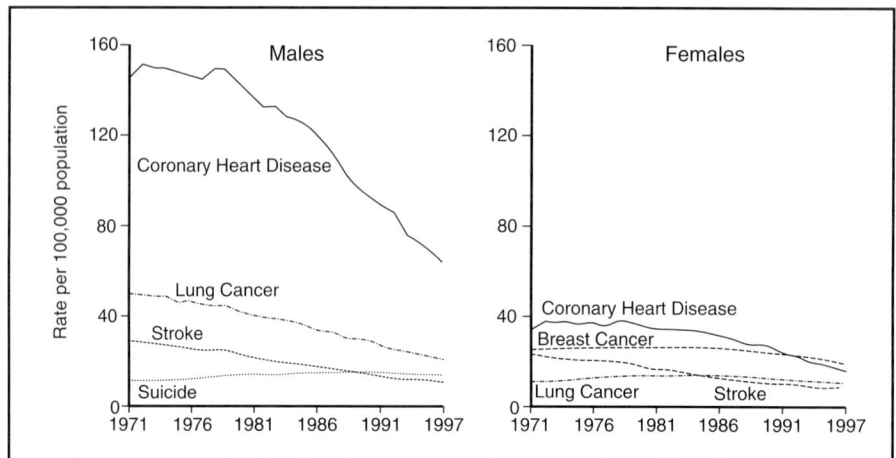

Cause of death in men and women in the UK

be more reluctant to visit a doctor. Although men take part in more sport than women, men still drink more than women and pay less attention to healthy eating. A worrying trend for men, particularly in Scotland, has been the rise in deaths from suicide. There have been various reasons put forward to explain this trend. Some say high unemployment and the associated loss of dignity and hope is a reason. Others say that the loss of the male identity as the 'breadwinner' has led to psychological problems for men to deal with as they grow up.

Regular* cigarette smoking among children: by gender and age

England				Percentages
	1982	1986	1992	1996
Males				
11	1	–	–	1
12	2	2	2	2
13	8	5	6	8
14	18	6	14	13
15	24	18	21	28
All males aged 11 to 15	11	7	9	11
Females				
11	–	–	–	–
12	1	2	2	4
13	6	5	9	11
14	14	16	15	24
15	25	27	25	33
All females aged 11 to 15	11	12	10	15

*Usually smoking at least one cigarette a week.
Source: Smoking Among Secondary School Children Survey, Office for National Statistics

While the numbers of adult smokers has been in decline since 1972, smoking is increasing among teenagers, especially teenage girls. By the age of 15, one third of all teenage girls now smoke and over one quarter of teenage boys are regular smokers.

There are various explanations for this trend. Some have pointed to pressures on young women not to become 'fat'. It is claimed that some teenage girls smoke in the belief that it stops cravings for junk food. Others have pointed to the successful advertising used by tobacco companies. Cigarettes retain an image of 'coolness' and sophistication. Despite the reality that cigarettes make your breath, hair and clothes smell, this clever marketing has worked.

ACTIVITIES

1 What evidence is there of differences between men's and women's health? Give at least three examples.
2 What reasons have been given for the increasing rates of suicide among young men?
3 Carry out a class survey on smoking. Do the evidence and the reasons given for smoking match the findings of the 'experts'?

POLITICAL REPRESENTATION

It was only in 1928 that all women won the right to vote. The overwhelming number of politicians across the world are male. For example, there has never been a female President of the USA. In Britain, we have had one female Prime Minister. Today, just over 18% of MPs are women, and 37% of Members of the Scottish Parliament (MSPs) are women. The 1997 General Election saw a massive increase in the numbers of women elected as MPs because the Labour Party made strong efforts to encourage women to be candidates. Britain moved from 50th to 24th in the world league of women in parliament. Today, out of our 659 MPs, 121 are female. In the Scottish Parliament, 48 MSPs are women, out of a total of 129.

OUR REPRESENTATIVES

	Local councillors (Scotland)	Members of Scottish Parliament (MSPs)	Members of Parliament (MPs)	Members of European Parliament (MEPs in Britain)
men	78%	63%	82%	76%
women	22%	37%	18%	24%

ACTIVITIES

What evidence is there to support the view that women are under represented at *all levels* in politics?

WHY SO FEW WOMEN REPRESENTATIVES?

On their way to the House of Commons or the Scottish Parliament, women face a number of hurdles.

The first is the familiar one of a woman's role within the family. As child rearers and home-makers, women have simply been too busy to attend meetings in the same way as men. In Britain there is a tradition of people 'serving their time' in political parties before being selected as a candidate for office. This will require lots of time attending meetings and preparing documents. Traditionally, these things have been much easier for men to do than women.

Secondly, there is the hurdle of being selected as a candidate. Politics is a dirty business! Many political meetings take place informally after the official meeting, in the pub. It is here that alliances and deals are made to put forward candidates for election. In the past, women have been excluded from these unofficial meetings. This may have been because women have not had the time to go to the pub after the meeting, or that the pubs have not been welcoming environments for women. There has been a tradition that politics is a 'man's job' and political parties have been slow to make efforts to select female candidates in constituencies (or 'seats') they expect to win. Many more women have been selected in seats that a party does not have a realistic chance of winning! The Labour Party has had a tradition of selecting a male candidate from a senior trade union background. The Conservatives have usually sought a male candidate from a successful business background.

The third hurdle is the traditional 'men's club' atmosphere of parliamentary politics. Although debates in the House of Commons are now controlled by the first ever female speaker, Betty Boothroyd, many of the traditions of the House emphasise the part played by males. The House of Commons voting procedures, often lasting into the small hours of the night, are more suited to males who may not have the same family commitments as women.

ACTIVITIES

1 Give three reasons why traditionally MPs have been more likely to be male than female.

Viewpoint A

"Women are making real progress in politics. We are seeing more and more women elected into important positions of responsibility. The opportunities for women to become Members of Parliament are greater than ever. This is thanks to the political parties making efforts to have more women MPs and also to changes in the working practices of Parliament."

Viewpoint B

"Little has changed in UK politics. The majority of our representatives continue to be men. There have been changes in the working practices of the Scottish Parliament, but parties are still more likely to select males rather than females as candidates. Until this changes, there will not be equal numbers of male and female MPs."

2 What differences are there between Viewpoint A and Viewpoint B?
3 Which viewpoint do you agree with and why?

Positive discrimination

Discrimination is usually used in a negative way, when a person or group is picked out for something bad to happen. However, it is possible to reverse a process by positively discriminating in favour of a particular group, who in the past have been negatively discriminated against. The aim, therefore, is to *positively discriminate* until the group has equal opportunities and status.

Between the years of 1992 and 1995, the Labour Party introduced positive discrimination in its selection of parliamentary candidates. It wanted to increase the number of female Labour MPs. Many male Labour MPs held 'safe seats'. A safe seat means that the MP has a comfortable majority of votes ahead of his/her nearest challenger. The political party knows it should retain this seat during the next election. Being selected as the political party's candidate for that seat is, therefore, the most important thing as the real election is probably a foregone conclusion. The following is a good example of a 'safe' Labour seat.

Constituency: Brentford and Isleworth (1997 General Election)

Mrs A Keen, Labour	32 249 votes
N. Deva, Conservative	17 825 votes
Dr G Hartwell, Liberal Democrat	4613 votes
J. Bradley, Green	687 votes

Labour majority: 14 424 votes

A decision was made by the Labour Party to 'positively discriminate' in *favour* of selecting women as candidates in these safe seats. The decision meant that if a male MP with a safe seat retired, a female candidate should be put forward in his place. This would continue until the number of female Labour MPs was the same as the number of males. In 1997, the number of female Labour MPs rose to 101 out of the total of 418 Labour MPs.

The other political parties recognised that they too could be doing more to encourage female candidates, but stopped short of Labour's positive discrimination. However, Labour's policy had to be abandoned before the 1997 General Election when a male member of the Labour Party, Peter Jepson, took the Labour Party to court. He claimed that under the Sex Discrimination Act, Labour's actions were discriminating against males. The Sex Discrimination Act protects men too! Jepson, supported by the Equal Opportunities Commission, won his case, but by the time positive discrimination was stopped, many women had already been selected as candidates in safe seats.

VIEWPOINTS IN FAVOUR OF POSITIVE DISCRIMINATION

1 It is necessary to enable women to catch up with men. Without this action, political parties will continue to select men as candidates and men will continue to dominate politics.
2 Merely encouraging parties to select women as candidates is not enough. The barriers of looking after children and homes mean that stronger action is needed to make sure that parties select women as candidates.
3 Before positive discrimination, change was too slow. Women have had the vote since 1928. Before Labour adopted positive discrimination, 91% of MPs were male.
4 Positive discrimination need only be a short-term measure. Once women have gained equal numbers to men, the practice can be stopped.

VIEWPOINTS AGAINST POSITIVE DISCRIMINATION

1 The best person should get the job, regardless of gender. Replacing one form of sex discrimination with another is no solution.
2 Positive discrimination is insulting to women. It suggests that women need the help of men to become MPs. Women are able to organise their lives for themselves and do not need this patronising help.
3 Positive discrimination makes women 'second class' MPs. People will believe that the woman only got the job 'because she is a woman' and not because of her ability.
4 It is insulting to male MPs that they cannot make good decisions on issues affecting women. Those who want to be MPs should be selected on their policies, not their gender.

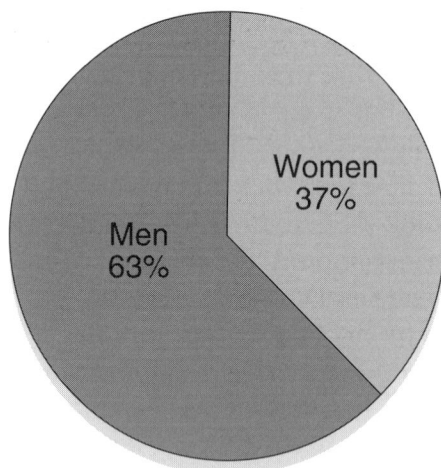

ACTIVITIES

1 Explain the term 'positive discrimination'.
2 Why was positive discrimination used by the Labour Party in the period 1992–1995?
3 Why was it stopped?
4 Outline the main arguments used for and against positive discrimination.
5 Which viewpoint do you agree with. Explain your answer.
6 Class debate: *"Given the amount of sexism that there still is in society, positive discrimination is necessary to enable women to get their fair share of the top jobs".*

THE SCOTTISH PARLIAMENT

In 1999, women gained 48 out of a total number of 129 seats in the new Scottish Parliament. As this translates to a figure of 37%, women are much nearer to equality in Scottish political life.

WHY DID THIS HAPPEN?

Firstly, the political parties made strong efforts to encourage women to stand as candidates. After positive discrimination was stopped, the Scottish Labour Party set up a policy of 'twinning'. This meant that a male standing for selection in one constituency should twin up with a female in another constituency and vice versa. This

Percentage of male and female MSPs

Men 63%
Women 37%

Female constituency MSPs, 1999: From left to right, Janis Hughes (Lab), Margaret Ewing (SNP) and Nora Radcliffe (Lib Dems)

Elected by the List system in 1999, Annabel Goldie, Conservative MSP for West of Scotland

ensured that there were equal numbers of male and female candidates standing for the Labour Party in Scotland. The other parties rejected this approach, but they all stood almost equal numbers of males and females as candidates.

Secondly, the working practices of the Scottish Parliament are more suitable for female MSPs. The Parliament only meets during school term times and strong efforts are made to have meetings during normal business hours, rather than in the evening.

Thirdly, the Additional Member voting system enabled many women of all parties to become 'List' MSPs. Under the voting system used by the Scottish Parliament, 56 MSPs were elected from party lists. This meant that voters, even more than usual, voted for a party, not a person. This meant that the old sexist excuse that 'voters don't like voting for women' could not be used.

The breakthrough made by women in the Scottish Parliament has been welcomed by all the political parties. Wendy Alexander of the Labour Party believes that women will be able to give a fresh insight into issues such as health, childcare, transport and drugs. Barbara Littlewood of Glasgow University, however, sees this election as a *'first step, but there is an awfully long way to go.'*

ACTIVITIES

1 What evidence is there that women made a breakthrough in the 1999 elections to the Scottish Parliament?
2 Give three reasons to explain why this happened.
3 In what ways may women, rather than men, be able to give a 'fresh insight' into issues such as health, childcare, transport and drugs?

RACE

THE ORIGINS OF RACISM

Let us suppose that you were a New Zealander or a Canadian who had never been to the British Isles and you happened to glance at the TV billings on any particular day. Two of the names you would almost certainly see are Trevor McDonald and Moira Stewart.

How do you account for the fact that both of these famous Scottish names belong to two of the best known and best loved black people in the UK? And that a quick glance through through any telephone directory in the Caribbean will turn up dozens of McPhersons, McGregors and Mackays, all of them with black faces? The answer lies in the history of the British slave trade.

It was a London company which initiated the trade that wrenched 12 million Africans away from the continent and plunged them into the hell of the slave plantations of the Americas. But the surnames suggest a wider responsibility.

As slaves were brought off the docks in Jamaica or any of the other islands, they were immediately stripped of their past clothes, family, identity. They would be forbidden to speak in their mother tongue. The most humiliating step of all would be to tell the slave that he or she no longer had an African name, and would be known henceforth by a European name.

The Scots were all too often the people who ran the cruellest part of the business – driving the slaves into higher and higher productivity. It was a vicious business – the average working life of a field hand in the West Indies was just eight years.

Trevor Phillips, journalist and broadcaster, Scotland on Sunday 10 October 1999

Ethnic minorities have been in Britain for a long time. Protestant refugees arrived from Central Europe in the 17th century. Irish and Jewish groups have settled since. Our most recent arrivals are refugees from the former Yugoslavia, Vietnam and the Middle East. Scots also have a history of living in other countries. There are more people of Scottish descent living outside of Scotland than in! That is what Rabbie Burns meant in his famous phrase, 'We're a' Jock Tamson's bairns'. He meant that people have always wandered the globe looking for happiness and a good standard of living. In doing this we have settled and mixed with other groups, each of us adding our own unique way of life to the country. Every January it would be possible to attend a Burns supper in almost any country in the world.

ACTIVITIES

1 Why do many black people have Scottish surnames?
2 Make a list of all the ethnic groups who have settled in Scotland.
3 What did Rabbie Burns mean by his phrase 'we're a' Jock Tamson's bairns'?
4 What evidence is there that Scots have settled all over the world?

For our purposes, the term 'ethnic minorities' will be used to describe people from the New Commonwealth and Pakistan, China, Africa, the West Indies, and their descendants who were born in Britain. The majority of today's ethnic minorities in the UK arrived in the 1960s. At that time there was no unemployment in the UK and there were serious shortages of workers in occupations such as transport. The Government actively recruited people from the countries of the former British Empire such as Pakistan, India and the islands of the West Indies, to do the jobs that white British people did not want. These incoming workers were subjected to vicious racism that stemmed from the stereotypes that began during the slave trade.

In the 18th and 19th centuries, many British businesses used the people of Africa, the Caribbean and Asia as slaves. The owners of these businesses believed themselves to be Christian and therefore felt guilty at the terrible injustices of slavery. They eased their conscience by inventing the racist idea of racial superiority. Because the white Europeans believed themselves to be superior, the other races were therefore inferior and could not expect the same rights as white people. Racial propaganda was spread which reflected other races as uncivilised, dirty or savage. It was no surprise, therefore, that white people in the UK reacted in a hostile manner to incoming groups in the 1960s, as the only stereotypes they had were negative and racist. The reality is that the majority of young Asian and black people today were born in the UK. They may have two identities, for example, Indian and British. Many Scots too have a similar dual nationality as Scottish and British.

Name	Aisha Ullah
Age	17
Place of birth	Kirkcaldy
Career plans	Business related, perhaps floristry
Religion	Muslim
National identity	Scottish
Hobbies	Working, watching TV, sleeping

Name	Gary McIntyre
Age	15
Place of birth	Edinburgh
Career plans	Police force
Religion	Christian (Church of Scotland)
National identity	Scottish
Hobbies	Football (Hibernian), golf

Name	Omar Rana
Age	14
Place of birth	Glasgow
Career plans	Don't know
Religion	Muslim
National identity	Scottish
Hobbies	Football

Name	Jeremy Klayman
Age	15
Place of birth	Edinburgh
Career plans	Acting
Religion	Jewish
National identity	Scottish
Hobbies	Football (Rangers)

Name	Michael Ford
Age	15
Place of birth	Glasgow
Career plans	Economics or politics
Religion	Roman Catholic
National identity	Scottish
Hobbies	Football (Celtic), music, computers

POPULATION OF THE UK

The 1991 census shows that just over 3 million (5.5%) of the 55 million people in Britain did not classify themselves as white.

ETHNIC POPULATION OF THE UK, 1991

In Scotland, proportionately fewer people are from ethnic minorities. According to the 1991 census, ethnic minorities account for 1.3% of Scotland's total population.

ETHNIC MINORITY GROUPS IN SCOTLAND

	Number	% of population of Scotland
Pakistani	21 192	0.42
Indian	10 050	0.2
Bangladeshi	1134	0.02
Chinese	10 476	0.21
Other Asian	4604	0.09
Black–African	2773	0.06
Black–Caribbean	934	0.02
Black–Other	2646	0.05
Other	8825	0.18
Total	**62 634**	**1.25**

People from ethnic minorities live in all parts of Scotland, but the majority live in Glasgow and Edinburgh. This is a common pattern throughout the world. Ethnic groups tend to settle next to people of a similar cultural background. In the USA, many Spanish-speaking Americans ('Hispanics') have settled in the state of California. Irish–Americans have settled in Boston. Scots, too, after the Highland clearances have settled in Nova Scotia (New Scotland), Canada. Scots in particular seem to be a close-knit group. We like to congregate together even when we leave the country for a few weeks! The numbers of Scottish bars in Majorca and Torremolinos indicate that we miss the company of our fellow Scots even when we want to get away from Scotland!

A MULTICULTURAL NATION

Scotland and the UK can accurately be described as multicultural. This means that we have many different races and religions, especially in our big cities. The vast majority of Britain's non-white population live in the large cities of England. London is the most multicultural of all our towns and cities. It has a vibrant mix of white ethnic minorities, e.g Turks and Greeks, and Asian minorities such as Bangladeshi, Pakistani, Indian and Chinese. 2% of Britain's non-white population live in Scotland. The largest group is Pakistani (21 200), followed by Chinese (10 476) and Indian (10 050). The 1991 survey did not ask a question about religion, but the CRE (Commission for Racial Equality), estimates that we have a multitude of different religions in the country:

Christian	40 million
Muslim	1–1.5million
Hindu	400 000–555 000
Jewish	300 000
Sikh	350 000–500 000
Buddhist	130 000
Jain	25 000–30 000
Zoroastrian	5000–10 000
Baha'I	6000
Jewish	300 000

ACTIVITIES

1 What evidence is there that Scotland is a 'multicultural nation'?

2 Describe the settlement pattern of people when they move to other countries.

3 What evidence is there that there is more than one national identity in Scotland?

4 Carry out a survey of pupils in your school. Your hypothesis is *"Young Scots today are more Scottish than British"*.
Make up three key questions that will allow you to answer whether or not your statement is true.
Make a note of when and where your survey was carried out. You should try for a sample of around 50 pupils.
Present your findings in bar or pie charts. Analyse your results.

Minority groups have also brought a variety of cultural traditions. Just as it would be a mistake to confuse the Scots with the English, it is a mistake to believe that all Asians share the same culture. In addition to English, Pakistani Scots may speak Urdu, the official language of Pakistan, and possibly Punjabi too. Indians from the Punjab state will speak Punjabi, and also possibly Hindi and/or Urdu. Those from Gujarat will speak Gujarati. Bangaladeshis are likely to speak Bengali. The Chinese in Scotland are most likely to speak in Cantonese or Hakka dialects.

Most of the minority groups from Pakistan, India and Bangladesh are Hindus, Sikhs or Muslims. There are also smaller religious groups from India, for example Jains, Buddhists, Christians and Parsees. It is difficult to generalise about the religious beliefs of the Chinese in Scotland, because many Chinese originate from the more westernised culture of Hong Kong.

Weblink: Britkid is at www.britkid.org

A GLOBAL VILLAGE

Increasingly, the world is becoming a smaller place. Instead of wishing that we all looked the same or believed in the same things, many people have come around to the idea that we now live in a global village. We should enjoy and respect our differences, while at the same time making sure that everyone has the same rights and responsibilities. For example, few would claim that life would be better without the multicultural food we can take advantage of. Here are just a few of the multicultural foods we can enjoy in Glasgow or Edinburgh.

- Scottish e.g. Haggis 'n' neeps
- French e.g. Coq au vin
- Indian e.g. Tandoori chicken
- Chinese e.g. Sweet and sour fried fish
- Jamaican e.g. Ackee and salt fish
- Cuban e.g. Rum glazed boniatos
- Moroccan e.g. Cous Cous
- Spanish e.g. Paella
- Mexican e.g. Tortilla
- Italian e.g. Rigatoni

Our lives would be the worse without the contributions made by the many Asian or Caribbean teachers, doctors, nurses, police officers or sports stars. It would be wrong to suggest that all people in Scotland and the UK are bigoted. There are plenty of examples of people from all backgrounds achieving success at work, in the media and in sport to suggest that the vast majority of us want equal opportunities for everyone.

We can fly to New York in eight hours. We can e-mail friends in New Zealand in seconds. The Internet can put us in touch with organisations and companies all over the world. Employers such as *McDonald's*, *Microsoft* and *Marconi* have offices in every continent. There is hardly a major football team that does not have star players from another country. Stereotypes and prejudices against people from different racial groups are out of date and irrelevant.

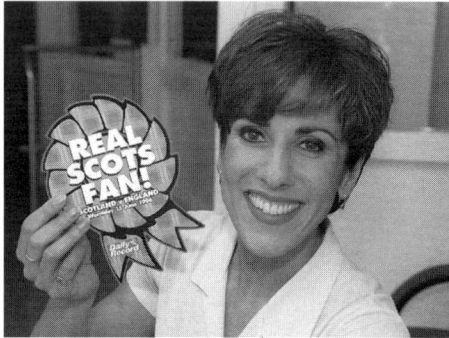

Shareen Nanjiani of Scotland Today

ACTIVITIES

1 Make a list of the foods from different cultures that you have tasted and enjoyed.
2 Give three reasons why it could be said that we now live in a global village.
3 Give examples from work, school or sport of Scotland in the global village.

Many Scots are proud of the country's reputation as a friendly place. Evidence would show that this, generally, is the case. In 1996 The Scottish Centre for Criminology carried out a survey on crime in Scotland. It interviewed 1182 adults in the former Strathclyde Region about their general concerns about crime and attitudes towards the police. It found that almost 70% of ethnic minorities said 'racial prejudice' was 'not a problem'. This still, however, leaves many people facing a needless problem and a hurdle to overcome in life.

Racism, therefore, remains a problem in Scotland. A study by the CRE in 1998 found that Scotland's ethnic minorities are more than three times as likely to suffer racist incidents as black and coloured people in England and Wales. Central Scotland had higher rates of racial incidents than any other area of the UK, 15 times higher than London.

"Every evening I get racial abuse because I will not serve drunk teenagers. I have seen them stealing sweets with my own eyes, but I

Mohammed Sarwar, MP for Glasgow Govan, Britain's first Muslim MP

can't search them or I will be called a child molester and if I do challenge them, I get racist abuse".

Fayyaz Muhammed, shop owner. Edited from an interview in Scotland on Sunday, *10 May 1999*

Racial abuse is not confined to 'visible' minority groups. The Irish have had to contend with negative stereotypes and discrimination for centuries. Many English people have been the objects of racial harassment. The parents of ecstasy victim Leah Betts considered moving away from Scotland because of anti-English abuse. Whilst trying to buy a croft on Skye, Paul and Jan Betts received a threatening letter saying that they would not be welcome in Scotland. One man called the couple 'southern English bastards'. Paul Betts described the author of the hate letter as a coward.

"We think most Scottish people are fantastic. We know this is not the way the Scots are. We have had a very good welcome from everyone else in Scotland."

Paul Betts, The Herald, *7 October 1998*

Anti-English, just like anti-Irish or anti-Scottish racism, is against the law.

ACTIVITIES

VIEWPOINT A

"Scotland is a friendly place. Scots welcome everyone, regardless of their colour, religion or ethnic background. Other countries may have a problem with racism, but we do not."

VIEWPOINT B

"Scotland is no different from any other country. It is no better and no worse. Racist attitudes are widespread."

1   What are the main differences between the two viewpoints?
2   To what extent can either, or both, of the viewpoints be guilty of exaggeration?
3   Which viewpoint do you agree with most. Give reasons for your answer.

LEGISLATION AGAINST RACISM

Like sexism, racial discrimination is illegal. The 1976 Race Relations Act makes racial discrimination a crime. It is an offence to discriminate in housing, in education and at work. If a person feels they have been discriminated against, they have the right to take the person or organisation responsible to court (or, if at work, to an industrial tribunal). It is also an offence to incite racial hatred through speeches or magazines. The 1998 Crime and Disorder Act introduced a new offence of racial harassment.

All people, not just non-white people, are protected by the Act. Most of the racial discrimination in Britain is against 'visible' minorities – people who 'look different'. However, white ethnic groups, such as Turks, Greeks, Irish, Scottish and English have felt racial discrimination at some point.

THE COMMISSION FOR RACIAL EQUALITY (CRE)

The CRE is comparable to the Equal Opportunities Commission (EOC). The CRE was set up in 1976 to try to make sure that the Race Relations Act was put into practice. Racism, like sexism, can be difficult to prove.

"The Commission for Racial Equality is working for a just society which gives everyone an equal chance to learn, work and live free from discrimination and prejudice, and from fear of racial harassment and violence."

The CRE has two main aims:

1 *To enforce the law.*
   It will help people who have complaints of racial discrimination. It can conduct investigations into companies where there is evidence of discrimination and can take action against unfair job advertisements.

2 *To promote equal opportunities and good race relations.*
   It will help companies to organise fair ways of running their business. It will advise government on improvements to existing laws and raise awareness within the public of race issues. It will also produce posters and leaflets to counter racial sterotypes or bullying.

Weblink: The Commission for Racial Equality is at www.cre.gov.uk

Like sexism, racism can be blatant and it can be subtle. There are three main types: direct, indirect and institutional.

DIRECT RACISM

This is when a person is directly treated less favourably because of his/her racial origins. Direct racial discrimination can come in many forms.

A Birmingham nightclub refused entry to a racially mixed group of people, claiming the club was full, yet it admitted groups of people who were all-white. A total of four discrimination claims were made against the nightclub and these were reported to the Commission for Racial Equality. The CRE supported the claims and a court fined the club £20,000.

> ### Black motorist stopped 34 times sues police
>
> In 1998, Carl Joseph, a butcher aged 27 who was stopped 34 times by police in two years, attempted to sue West Midlands police for racial harassment. Mr Joseph lost the case. The trouble started in 1992 when Mr Joseph was arrested while driving a van and detained on suspicion of being a banned motorist. After being held in a cell for one and a half hours he was released when police admitted their mistake. When he complained, he was sent a cheque for £250 by West Midlands Police. He claimed that after this time, he was racially harassed by the police.
>
>
>
> Mr Jones, who has no convictions and a clean driving licence, claimed that the police threatened to plant drugs in his car after he complained about being stopped so often. He has been forced to sell his distinctive red Metro with the words "One Love" on the side.

Racial harassment is a serious problem. Name calling, bullying and 'jokes' are the most obvious. Assault and intimidation often come next. In Scotland, in 1997/98, the police recorded 1097 racial incidents – a 35% increase from the 811 incidents the previous year. All racially motivated crimes are recorded by the police, but many people do not go to the police for every 'joke' or insult that is made. Similarly, many people may be harassed but not claim that there was a racial motive. The reality, therefore, is that racial harassment is likely to be more widespread than the official statistics indicate. The figures are likely to be the tip of the iceberg.

Racism and football

Black footballers are commonplace today. Stars such as Rod Wallace or Andy Cole are idolised by thousands. Racial abuse of black players has become a lot less common. Actions by clubs inside football grounds mean that racist taunts are no longer tolerated. This was not always the case. The first black footballers in Britain, such as Clyde Best of West Ham and Cyrille Regis of West

ACTIVITIES

1 What are the laws which try to ensure equal opportunities for different racial groups?
2 Explain the aims of the Commission for Racial Equality.
3 Do you feel that Carl Joseph has been the victim of racial harassment? Give reasons for your answer.
4 Why might official figures for racial harassment be the 'tip of the iceberg'?

Clyde Best, a role model for black footballers

Bromwich Albion, were subjected to terrible racist attacks. Paul Wilson of Celtic in the 1970s and Mark Walters of Rangers, as recently as the 1980s, were the targets of mindless abuse. The players admit that *on* the field this made no difference, in fact, the abuse made them try all the harder, but off the field, racism continued.

In his autobiography, John Barnes writes of how he has spent his adult life battling with racism as a player with Watford, Liverpool, Newcastle United, Charlton Athletic and also as an England international player.

"Every day as I drove through Eltham to Charlton's training ground I passed the spot where Stephen (Lawrence) was killed. People used to say to me 'be careful when you go out around here'. But what happened to Stephen Lawrence could have happened anywhere in London. Even before I moved to Merseyside, there were slogans like LIVERPOOL ARE WHITE daubed on the stadium walls. I received letters from sad old men apoplectic that blacks should represent Liverpool, and bananas were thrown at me. Everton fans spat at me, threw bananas and chanted 'Niggerpool, Niggerpool, Niggerpool'. Racism is a way of life for black people. The majority of motorists stopped by Merseyside Police are black. When I played for Liverpool, my car was often flagged down."

The Professional Footballers Association, along with the CRE, organise a very successful campaign 'Kick Racism out of Football'. It seeks to encourage footballers from all racial and ethnic groups to play and watch football in an atmosphere free from racial abuse. Rather than simply lecture fans about how bad it is to be a racist, it seeks to educate young people on how ethnic minorities have added to the quality of football and how dull the game could be without their contribution. It also seeks to encourage clubs to attract a wider group of fans, because ethnic minorities had stayed away from grounds due to fear of racial abuse.

In Scotland, neither the Scottish Football Association or the Scottish PFA have organised an anti-racist campaign, although they have supported the English campaign. It has been the responsibility of individual clubs. Celtic launched Bhoys against Bigotry in 1995 as an effort to combat racism and the problem of religious hatred (sectarianism) among football fans.

It has long been a myth that Scotland's Asian community are not interested in football. In 1998 the Government set up a football task force to investigate what could be done about racism in football. It was shocked at what it found. 65% of Asian players said they had experienced racism. 50% of Asians who played in all-Asian teams did so because of fear of racism. 55% of professional clubs in Britain thought that football 'was not popular with Asians' and 69% of professional club officials thought that Asian footballers were 'physically less suited than other racial groups'. In fact a survey by the Sports Council in 1991 showed that 60% of Bengali boys

The UK Asian Football Championships

played football along with 42% of Pakistanis and 33% of Chinese boys. When asked 'What single thing would attract more Asian spectators to football matches', most Asians replied 'an Asian professional'.

In September 1999, the first ever UK Asian Football Championships was held at Celtic Park. The event was organised by Celtic, Glasgow Sports Council and the Scottish Asian Sports Association. In the final, Albion Sports of Bradford beat Azaad Sports of Wolverhampton 4–2. Presenting the trophy, Celtic coach John Barnes commented:

"There were 40 year old guys out there acting like kids and, for me, that is what football is all about. Twenty years ago we were asking 'When are black players going to break through?' and you can see how many there are now, so I consider it only a matter of time before Asian players begin making their mark. It's important that young Asian kids have their own heroes to look up to and, once that happens, I think the norm will be not Asian Championships, but just British championships with Asians playing alongside whites, blacks and whoever."

Weblink: Kick Racism out of Sport is at www.kickitout.org

ACTIVITIES

"Asians are not interested in playing football." Statement by Tom Brown. Give two pieces of evidence to show that Tom Brown is being selective in his use of facts.

INDIRECT RACISM

This is where racism is not applied directly against someone, but is dealt more subtly. For example, an industrial tribunal found a Liverpool store manager guilty of indirect racism. He had told the careers office that he did not want job applications from certain parts of town. As these parts of town were areas that ethnic minorities were likely to live, the tribunal ruled that this was a case of indirect racism.

EXTENDED WRITING

Discuss the view that racism is still a problem in Scottish sport.

INSTITUTIONAL RACISM

Institutional racism is the result of attitudes that may exist within an organisation. It may be what the organisation does, but also what it does not do. Like indirect sexism, it may arise because informal practices exclude certain groups. For example, it is often the case that a person gains promotion because of social contacts ("it's not what you know, but who you know"). This process of 'networking', whereby people make informal business contacts at sport or social evenings, is commonplace. A white male is more likely to have a 'network' of important contacts, perhaps through a golf club, than women or ethnic minorities. Institutional racism may therefore take place unconsciously because the organisation may be ignorant of the way in which it recruits or promotes people.

Stephen Lawrence

Doreen and Neville Lawrence

RACE AND CRIME

"What I see is that black people are still dying on the streets and in the back of police vans." Doreen Lawrence

The murder of Stephen Lawrence in 1993 was a wake up call to the country about direct and institutional racism. Stephen Lawrence, an 18 year old black A-level student, was stabbed to death in a racially motivated attack in London by white youths on 22 April 1993.

The five white youths accused of Stephen's murder were not convicted due to a lack of evidence.

For a long time there has been mistrust and bad feelings between the Metropolitan Police and the black community. In 1981 there was serious rioting in Brixton, South London. In 1985, a police officer was hacked to death in a riot on a black council estate in Tottenham, North London. The man found guilty of PC Blakelock's murder, Wilson Silcott, has always claimed his innocence and that he was 'stitched up' by the police. The inquest into the Stephen Lawrence investigation, led by Sir William MacPherson, found that 'unwitting institutional racism' existed within the Metropolitan Police. It concluded that the officers investigating Stephen Lawrence's murder did not apply the same professionalism to the case as they would have done towards the murder of a white youth.

Until recently, the police were exempt from the Race Relations Act. It was not until 2000 that the Labour Government passed an amendment to the Act which made the police subject to the same laws of the land as every other public organisation.

The Chief of the Metropolitan Police, Sir Paul Condon, apologised to the Lawrence family for the poor quality of the police investigation, but he would not concede that the Metropolitan Police was 'institutionally racist'. He claimed that the attitudes of his

The suspects in the Stephen Lawrence murder case

officers were typical of the attitudes in society. The MacPherson report spoke of 'unwitting racism' within the police force, meaning that many officers did not realise that they were discriminating against minority groups. MacPherson criticised the racist 'canteen culture' within the police force which made jokes and certain assumptions about the black community. In Scotland in 1995, the Chief of Strathclyde Police, Leslie Sharp, made a racist joke about a black robot at an after-dinner party. He later apologised.

The 1991 census figure shows that 5.5% of the UK population are of a 'ethnic minority' background. In 1999, The Metropolitan Police had less than 4% of its officers from ethnic minorities, yet London has a higher proportion of people from the minorities. Since the MacPherson report, the Metropolitan Police has more actively sought to recruit black and Asian police officers and is making strong efforts to end the 'canteen culture'.

The Metropolitan Police has taken honest and serious efforts to counter racism. This has included:

1 Racism Awareness meetings with all police officers. During these meetings, police officers speak honestly about their experiences with representatives from ethnic minority communities. They explain that it is a hard job being a police officer and that often the police are on the receiving end of abuse too. Even so, the 'canteen culture has been challenged'. Anti-racism officers have been appointed to make police officers aware of the scale of the problem. London has 260 000 police officers. Even if only 1% of these officers are racist, if they have 10 racist encounters per day, that amounts to 2600 racist incidents every day!

2 The Metropolitan Police has made strong efforts to improve relations with ethnic minority communities. Adverts have been placed in newspapers to encourage more recruits from minority groups.

The MacPherson report highlighted the mistrust that exists between the ethnic community and the police force. According to Home

Office findings, 23% of Caribbeans claimed to have been stopped by the police, compared to 16% of white people and 15% of Asians. Overall black people were five times more likely to be stopped and searched than whites.

The 1996 British Crime Survey showed a total of 19 million crimes committed in England and Wales. The figures also showed that ethnic minorities, especially Pakistanis and Bangladeshis, were much more likely to be the victims of crime than other groups. The main reason to explain this is that ethnic minorities tend to be more likely than whites to live in dangerous inner city areas.

Fear of crime was also greatest among ethnic minorities. While only one in 15 white people were afraid of being attacked because of their skin colour, the figure rose to one in three for people from ethnic minorities. Despite the high proportion of successful footballers from ethnic minorities, 26% of people from ethnic minorities avoided matches because of fear of crime or violence. This was double the number of whites.

In cases of violent robbery, half of all white victims of mugging said all the offenders were white and one third said all the offenders were black. Black offenders were much more likely to mug other blacks or Asian people.

THE SCOTTISH EXPERIENCE

In Scotland, relations between the police and the ethnic minority community appear to be much better. The 1996 Strathclyde survey showed that white attitudes towards the police were less positive than ethnic minority attitudes. When asked the question 'Do the majority of police in Scotland do a good job?', 78% of Indians said 'Yes', compared with 76% of whites. The survey did not show any major differences between whites and members of ethnic minority groups in crime-related matters and contact with the Scottish police.

This does not mean that racial harassment is not a serious issue in Scotland. In 1997, Scottish teenager Imran Khan was murdered by a racist gang in Glasgow, a murder very similar to the Stephen Lawrence tragedy. In 1998, a Glasgow police constable, Lawrence Ramadas, successfully sued Strathclyde Police for racial discrimination. Between April 1998 and April 1999 Strathclyde Police recorded 337 racial incidents.

There does, however, appear to be a greater awareness of the potential for racial discrimination in Scotland. The race relations policy put into practise by Chief Constable John Orr of Strathclyde Police is widely seen to be a model of good policing. There has been a strong attempt to recruit young Asian people into the police. MARIM (Multi Agency Racial Incident Monitoring) groups have been set up. These involve not just police, but social workers, housing officers and education personnel to tackle problems in communities. Because these groups have won the confidence of the

How To Report A Racial Incident

Fife Constabulary seek to encourage the reporting of all Racial Incidents and Police Officers in the Force are given training in the sensitive area of Race Relations.

Incidents Of A Racial Nature

A Racially motivated incident is defined as:

(i) Any incident in which it appears to the Reporting or Investigating Officer that the complaint involves an element of Racial Motivation.

(ii) Any incident which includes an allegation of Racial Motivation made by any person.

A Racial Incident can include a physical attack, vandalism, threatening, abusive or insulting words or behaviour, graffiti, etc.

Action To Be Taken By Members Of The Public

(i) If you are a victim of a Racial Incident, or witness a Racial Incident, report the matter immediately to your Local Police Station or any Police Officer.

(ii) If the offender is unknown to yourself, it will be helpful if you can give an accurate description of the offender to the Police. It will also be helpful if you give a motive for the incident if known.

(iii) You should make a note of the details, which will enable you to refer to your complaint at a later stage, if necessary.

(iv) **REMEMBER** in an emergency, telephone the free service **'999'** and ask for the Police and if required an Ambulance or the Fire Brigade.

ACTION TO BE TAKEN BY THE POLICE

(i) All Officers are required to give priority to such incidents subject to the seriousness of the alleged complaint.

(ii) The Officer attending a Racial Incident is required to submit a special report and this report is monitored at local level and also at Police Headquarters by the Assistant Chief Constable.

(iii) The Officer will keep you, the victim, updated as to the progress of your complaint and where appropriate give you advice on personal and property security.

(iv) You may also be referred to your Local Victim Support Scheme if appropriate.

As a matter of General Policy, Fife Constabulary is opposed to the concept of Racism and you will help us to achieve this if you report every such incident to the Police.

Racial harassment is taken seriously by Fife Constabulary

ethnic minority community, more racist crimes have been reported and acted on.

The discrimination case by PC Lawrence Ramadas was a setback to good race relations, but rather than deny that a problem existed, as happened in the Stephen Lawrence enquiry, John Orr swiftly made a public apology. He offered PC Ramadas financial compensation and his job back. This was accepted and welcomed by the ethnic minority community. Strathclyde Police has investigated six complaints of racism by police officers.

As Scottish Home Affairs Minister Henry McLeish commented *"racism is not just something which affects the police – it affects Scottish society as a whole. There must be no complacency in this area."*

The Herald, *25 February 1999*

ACTIVITIES

1 Explain what is meant by institutional racism. Give examples.
2 What evidence is there that relations between the Metropolitan Police and the black community are tense?
3 What was the main conclusion of the MacPherson report into the murder of Stephen Lawrence?
4 What steps have the Metropolitan Police taken to counter racism within the organisation?

Extended writing

5 What evidence is there **for** and **against** the view that racism is less of a problem within the Scottish police? Overall, do you agree with this view. Give reasons to support your answer.

RACE AND WORK

As we have already seen, ethnic minority groups were encouraged to come to the UK because there were too many jobs available. Today's generation of Asians and Caribbeans are British and have the same rights and responsibilities as other British citizens. Evidence would also show that ethnic minority groups are more likely to be unemployed. In 1995/96, the unemployment rate for people from ethnic minorities was more than double the rate for white people.

Unemployment rates are highest among those with fewest qualifications.

Unemployment rates, averages for June 1995–May 1996

| | Working age (16–59/64) | | |
	all %	men %	women %
All groups	9	10	7
White	8	9	6
Non-White	18	20	16
Black Caribbean	19	22	16
Black African	28	27	29
Black Other	20	*	21*
Black mixed	22	*	*
Indian	12	13	11
Pakistani	26	26	25
Bangladeshi	33	26	*
Chinese	*	*	*
Other	15	17	11

* numbers under 6,000; estimates not included
Source: Labour Force Survey, Summer 1995–Spring 1996

However, a CRE study showed that racial inequality continues even for those with university degrees. In 1998, 11% of black people and 6% of Asians were unemployed, compared with 3% of white degree holders.

Young people experienced the worst unemployment. Within this group of people, young women were much more likely to be unemployed. Young black women were four times more likely to be unemployed than young white women.

To counter racial discrimination, many companies now have an Equal Opportunities Policy. This means that the company will make it clear that jobs within the company are open to everyone in the community. The company will also check whether minority groups are gaining jobs and promotion within the organisation and will take action against any racism – direct, indirect or institutional. Some companies, such as the Metropolitan Police will take 'proactive' steps, such as job adverts, to recruit more people from minority backgrounds.

The experience of unemployment, or negative racial attitudes within work places, has meant that many ethnic minorities have started up their own businesses. The local shop owned by a Pakistani or Indian family is commonplace in Scotland. The strong family ties in these communities have been a factor, but there is a strong economic explanation. In the retail world of supermarkets and out-of-town malls, owning a grocer shop is a time-consuming business. Profit margins on goods are low. In order to make a living, shop owners have to put in long and often antisocial hours. Many white Scots have not been prepared to put in the long hours required to make a profit in the corner shop business.

In February 1999, *The Independent* newspaper carried out a survey of major employers in Britain. *Virgin*, *Railtrack* and *BT* categorically denied having 'institutional racism'. All the others, such as *McDonald's*, *Marks & Spencer*, the *BBC* and *British Airways*, all had long-standing equal opportunities policies.

RACE AND SOCIAL ISSUES: EDUCATION

Ethnic minority groups have seen many improvements in education. In co-operation with the CRE and local authority Equal Opportunity officers, schools in Scotland have clear equal opportunities policies. The benefits to pupils are that racist bullying is taken very seriously. The employment of professionally-trained teachers of English as an Additional Language has meant that pupils with language needs can receive additional help. Across all subjects,

IF THIS IS A PAKI, A DARKIE AND A CHINKY YOU'RE A RACIST.

1997 european year

Edinburgh will not tolerate racial harassment. against racism

Racist bullying is not tolerated in schools

from CDT to English, teachers are made aware of the opportunities to appreciate the unique educational contribution pupils from all backgrounds can make.

Inequalities do continue though. A CRE study in England and Wales showed that in 1997, more than one in five people among ethnic minorities had no qualifications compared with around 18% of white people.

This figure does not, however, reveal the changes that have taken place in recent years. As ethnic groups have become more confident with the English language and generations have grown up in the UK, a greater proportion of ethnic minority students are receiving education and training than in the white community.

On the other hand, in 1995/96, black Caribbean pupils were five times as likely as white pupils to be permanently excluded from school. Out of these figures, eight out of 10 pupils excluded were boys aged between 12 and 15.

ACTIVITIES

1 Describe the efforts that have been made to counter racism at school.
2 *"Schools have been very successful in creating equal opportunities in education."*
Give reasons **for** and **against** this point of view. Overall, does the evidence support the point of view?

RACE AND POLITICAL REPRESENTATION

Just as women are under-represented in decision making, Britain's ethnic minorities are lacking a presence in the corridors of power. The 1997 British General election showed a total number of nine MPs from an ethnic background. In the elections to the Scottish Parliament in 1999, not one MSP came from an ethnic minority background. In local government, there are a total of just seven councillors from the black and Asian communities.

"The exclusion from the Scottish Parliament of people from black and minority ethnic communities, the majority of whom were born here, is a deplorable statement of how they are valued here. We have been 'ethnically cleansed'."
Bashir Maan, Scotland's first ever Asian local councillor in 1974

	Local Councillors in Scotland	Members of Scottish Parliament (MSPs)	Members of Parliament (MPs): UK figure	Members of European Parliament (MEPs): UK figure
White European	1215	129	650	84
Black/Asian	7 (0.5%)	0 (0%)	9 (1.3%)	3(3%)

Why?

Like women, ethnic minorities have to overcome a number of hurdles in order to achieve equal representation.

Firstly, there is a lack of role models. There are few high profile politicians from an ethnic background. This means that white Scots see an ethnic politician as something unusual. They see the skin colour, rather than seeing the person as an individual. It also means that younger ethnic minorities see politics as being something which only white Scots do. Mohammed Sarwar became Britain's first ever Muslim MP when he was elected as Labour MP for Glasgow Govan in 1997. This proves that candidates from ethnic minorities can be elected and that the voice of minorities will be listened to by the political parties.

A second hurdle is the language problem. When ethnic minorities first settled in Scotland it took some time to learn the language. Many Scots do not speak English the way it is pronounced in language textbooks! A number of people in England watch Rab C Nesbitt with subtitles in order to understand it! Minority groups were too concerned with settling into a new country, finding a home, establishing a business and finding schools to be concerned with politics. Change is, however, taking place – the new generation are proud of their ethnic and Scottish background.

Thirdly, racism must also be seen as a factor. While it is difficult to prove, the fact that not one black or Asian candidate was placed in a 'safe seat' or at the top of a party list shows that institutional racism could be present in all the major political parties. Perhaps the parties fear that voters may be racist and not vote for a black or Asian candidate. There is no doubt that the result from the Scottish Parliament was a setback. Najimee Parveen of the Commission for Racial Equality in Scotland is extremely concerned that Scotland's new parliament started off as an all-white institution: *"The parties must be seen to be genuinely interested in increasing black and minority participation. It seems to be happening for women, but not for black and ethnic minorities"*.

In the UK Parliament a new scheme has been introduced by the three main political parties to attract more minority MPs. Twenty-two black and Asian representatives have been selected to 'shadow' MPs from the party of their choice. They will follow the MP round the House of Commons, learning what an MP does and picking up the skills required to stand as a candidate and be a good MP if elected. Jasvinder Sanghera (34) sees the opportunity to shadow a Labour MP as a chance to gain experience: *"I want to be an MP and this is like a foot in the door."*

ACTIVITIES

1 Give two reasons why the election of Mohammed Sarwar as MP for Glasgow Govan was a breakthrough for ethnic minorities in Scotland.
2 Explain the three reasons why there are so few black and Asian representatives.
3 What steps could political parties take to achieve a fairer number of ethnic minority representatives?

HEALTH AND WEALTH

This chapter looks at four main areas of **Equality in Society** and will:

◆ explain the ideas behind the welfare state and discuss the challenges facing government support for the 'socially excluded' in the new millennium

◆ examine the reasons for poverty in the UK and the effects it has for those living on a low income

◆ examine the health needs of different groups of people in the UK and the different forms of health care available

In addition, there are two case studies of different groups in society: lone parents and the elderly

THE WELFARE STATE

The 20th century has seen the state, or the government, taking on responsibility for the welfare of its citizens. Before this time, the attitude can be summed up by the French term 'laissez faire', meaning 'leave alone'. In other words, the government that worked best was the one that did least.

Unfortunately, this approach did not provide health and wealth for everyone in the UK. The Victorian rich were well educated, had a good standard of living, and could live a happy retirement. The poor, on the other hand, suffered a wretched existence. The only hospitals that would treat them were dirty, dangerous and frightening places. With a lack of anaesthetics and untrained, often drunk staff, few people entered hospital willingly. Young children would be kept from school in order to go out and work. This lack of education ensured that a low paid, unskilled job would be the best that could be hoped for. There was no pension in old age. Most of the poor worked until they died. The elderly poor were cooped up in old warehouses along with the mentally ill.

The Liberal Government of 1908 was shocked at the degree of poverty and introduced the first reform which led to the welfare state. The Government promised pensions for those on low incomes, over the age of 70, who had a good work record and 'moral character'.

A number of other benefits followed, until, after World War Two, the Labour Government promised a 'comprehensive system' to provide security for all 'from cradle to the grave'. The inspiration for this came from the report of the **Beveridge Commission** of 1944. The war had brought the country together. The middle classes in the countryside had met the inner city poor for the first time. Rather than meeting dirty, immoral creatures as they had expected, they felt pity for the poor. The poor had the same aspirations as them. They wanted education, work, a decent house, to do well for their children and to have a happy, healthy retirement. The wartime spirit brought about a 'collective' response to the nation's problems; there was a shared belief or consensus that the whole country should work together to meet the needs of the people. This meant the introduction of a comprehensive welfare state.

THE FIVE SOCIAL GIANTS

Beveridge identified five giant evils of society which he wanted to end: squalor (poor housing), ignorance (lack of education), idleness (unemployment), want (poverty) and disease (poor health).

The incoming Labour Government and successive governments until 1979 saw it as their task to win the war against these five evils. In the period between 1945 and 1979, the 'post-war consensus' between the main political parties was that it was the role of government to provide for those who could not provide for themselves.

SQUALOR

The slum houses of the big cities were torn down and replaced with council housing at affordable rents. New estates were built on the periphery of the big cities. 'New Towns' were built in Scotland, such as East Kilbride, Livingstone, Irvine, Glenrothes and Cumbernauld.

IGNORANCE

The school leaving age was gradually increased to 16 and the '11-plus' exam was ended. This exam was an entrance test for high school that pupils took at the age of 11. Those who passed went to 'the high school', those who didn't went to the 'dovey school'. The wealthy meanwhile could go to private, fee-paying schools. Government wanted to end this division. 'Comprehensive' schools were set up, run by government, for all children from 11–16.

IDLENESS

The war effort had brought about full employment, i.e. a job was available for everyone who was able to work. Post-war governments believed they had conquered the evil of unemployment and all the social miseries it caused. The Government 'nationalised' many of the private companies; for example 'British Rail', 'British Coal', 'British Gas' and 'British Steel' were all set up. As the Government was now the major employer in the country, it believed it could control the amount of jobs available.

WANT

As unemployment had been conquered, the Government set up a comprehensive range of benefits for the young, the old, and those of working age who were unable to work.
The benefits included the following:
◆ child benefit
◆ sickness benefit

◆ housing benefit
◆ disability benefit
◆ state retirement pension.

These were described as 'cradle to the grave' benefits. In fact, the individual was looked after even before and after the grave. Free maternity classes were available for mothers to be, and if a person could not afford their own funeral, the state provided!

DISEASE

The National Health Service was set up in 1948. This replaced the previous patchwork care available for low income families. The NHS aimed to provide health care for all, regardless of income, free at the point of use. It aimed not just to treat the sick, but to promote good health, in the belief that 'prevention is better than cure'.

ACTIVITIES

1   Describe health care for the poor before the welfare state.
2   What was meant by care from the 'cradle to the grave'?
3   Match up the five giant evils of Beveridge with their proposed solutions:

Giant evil	Solution
Ignorance	Full employment
Want	Comprehensive education
Disease	Cradle to the grave benefits
Squalor	The National Health Service
Idleness	Council housing

WHERE WAS THE MONEY TO COME FROM?

Post-war governments funded the welfare state in two main ways: National Insurance and taxation.

NATIONAL INSURANCE

National Insurance would be a deduction from the wages of all those who worked. From an individual point of view, the government believed that people would not object to paying, as the individual themselves had benefited from an early age. The person would also have a 'safety net' to fall back on if they lost their job, and could look forward to a state pension on retirement. From a national point of view, the system was based like any other form of insurance. So long as more people were paying into the pool of money than were claiming, the government could afford to run the welfare state.

TAXATION

There are two main forms of taxation: direct taxes and indirect taxes. Direct taxes are deducted by the Inland Revenue from wages. The post-war consensus believed in the principle of 'progressive taxation' – the more a person earned, the more they paid in direct taxation.

Indirect taxes are those placed on goods and services, such as VAT or duty on fuel, alcohol and cigarettes. The government believed that the majority of people supported the principle of progressive taxation, as they had the benefits of the welfare state. As for VAT, these goods were seen to be a choice, and individuals only paid the tax if they chose to purchase these 'luxuries'.

ACTIVITIES

1 Describe the difference between direct and indirect taxes.
2 Which type of tax do you prefer? Give reasons for your answer.
3 Look up the views of the political parties on the Internet. Whose views do you agree with most? Give reasons for your answer.

www.labour.org.uk
www.libdems.org.uk
www.scottishgreens.org.uk
www.scotsocialistparty.org.uk
www.snp.org.uk
www.tory.org.uk

THE CHALLENGE TO THE WELFARE STATE

The welfare state today is the subject of a furious row between the political parties. The Conservative governments of 1979–1997 changed a great deal of the ways in which government dealt with the five giants. The Conservatives would like to cut back spending on the welfare state and encourage people to look after their own health and social security needs. The New Labour Government has promised a 'modernisation' of the welfare state to equip it for the new millennium. It would like to cut certain benefits to some people and increase benefits for other groups of people. The Liberal Democrats have supported the Government in most areas, but have disagreed over cuts in Disability Benefit. The Scottish National Party believes that Scots have different welfare needs and wants from other parts of the UK. Other parties in the Scottish Parliament, such as the Green Party and the Scottish Socialist Party, have strong views too. They would like to see spending on the welfare state increased and spending on other areas, such as defence, decreased.

WHY THE CHALLENGE?

The challenge to the welfare state came from three directions: economically, socially and politically.

Economic factors
High unemployment
Beveridge assumed that there would always be full employment in the UK and that National Insurance contributions and taxation from these people would pay for the welfare state. This has not happened.

The 1980s saw unemployment rise to over three million. For a long time there has been a hard core of long-term unemployed people who have never worked. This means a huge loss to the Government in people paying *into* the welfare pool, and a huge drain *out* of the system in benefits claims. Unemployment is a 'double whammy'. There is also a very strong link between unemployment and other social problems.

The decline of labour intensive industry

A second reason is the changes that have taken place at work. The labour market of the new millennium is far removed from that of the post-war period. More women are working and expect to work. In Beveridge's day, work was a male activity. Scotland relied on huge 'labour intensive' industries such as coal, steel, ship-building and other manufacturing. These were seen to be, and often were, 'jobs for life'. Sons followed their father into the shipyard or the pit. These industries are now gone. They have been replaced by privately-owned, computer-based service industries. These industries are often multinational. This means that they have workplaces all over the world, and feel no strong loyalties to a particular community. They do not provide 'jobs for life'. Working life is insecure and sometimes temporary. Having a job depends not on masculinity, but on having skills and a flexible approach to change.

The labour market has grown in size and more individuals have been out of work, often for very long periods. The creators of the welfare state did not foresee this happening.

Social factors

Increase in life expectancy

Firstly, Beveridge believed that the success of the welfare state would lead to fewer claims on the system. The opposite has happened. The welfare state is a victim of its own success. There are now more elderly people than ever. The average life expectancy for men born in 1900 was 45; now it is 74. For women, the average has risen from age 50 in 1900 to 79 now. In Scotland, it is estimated that one in five of the population will be elderly in 2021. People are living longer, partly because there has been an absence of the world wars that killed millions in the years 1914–1945, but also because the NHS has worked. Improvements in housing and in public health generally have meant an increase in life expectancy for all. This is a cause for celebration. But it has to be paid for.

Changes in family life

Secondly, family life has changed considerably since 1945. Changes in divorce laws and the decline in influence of the church have meant a growth in lone-parent families. Beveridge assumed that the 'nuclear' family of married parents and children would be the norm. Since the war this domestic arrangement has been in decline. Co-habitation and lone-parent families are increasingly common. This has meant increasing demands on the welfare state, as the system was designed to meet the needs of the nuclear family.

Political factors

The Thatcher revolution

The Thatcher revolution of 1979–1990 reflected the changes that had been going on in society. The Government also created the basis for a new social attitude towards work and the welfare state.

Those *in* work in the 1980s saw their incomes rise. The sale of council houses gave many their own home for the first time. The sale of the house brought wealth they had only dreamt of. Many others made money through house sales during the boom years. The Conservatives privatised the industries that Labour had nationalised. Many made money through the buying and selling of shares in British Telecom and British Steel. While unemployment and poverty rose in communities which relied on the 'old' industries, incomes rose for those in the thriving private sector businesses of construction, banking, new technology and catering.

The Conservatives encouraged *individual* solutions instead of collective ones.

	Collective solution	Individual solution
Housing	Council housing	Private housing
	Rents to local authorities	Mortgages to banks
Education	State schooling	Independent schooling
	Student grants	Student fees
Unemployment	Government help	Individual to take initiative
	Skillseeker or New Deal	Take out career loan
Poverty	State benefits	Private insurance
	State pension	Occupational and/or private pension
Health	National Health Service	Private medical insurance

A new generation of voters came into existence. Born from the mid 1970s onwards, this generation had not known the misery of the pre-welfare society. The generation of so-called 'Thatcher's children' had opportunities to have a very good standard of living, especially if their parents had done well from the Thatcher Government. This generation had new political priorities. The post-war consensus of government 'tax and spend' was gone. Any political party who ran for election promising tax increases to pay for welfare was easily beaten.

Gordon Brown, Chancellor of the Exchequer, 1999 Budget speech

NEW LABOUR AND THE WELFARE STATE

New Labour is adamant that it does not wish to end the welfare state, but to 'modernise' it.

"We will guarantee that people in need get decent support, but we expect that people who can, should help to provide for themselves. The best way out of poverty is work. We aim to make work pay."

WELFARE TO WORK

A way out of the poverty trap

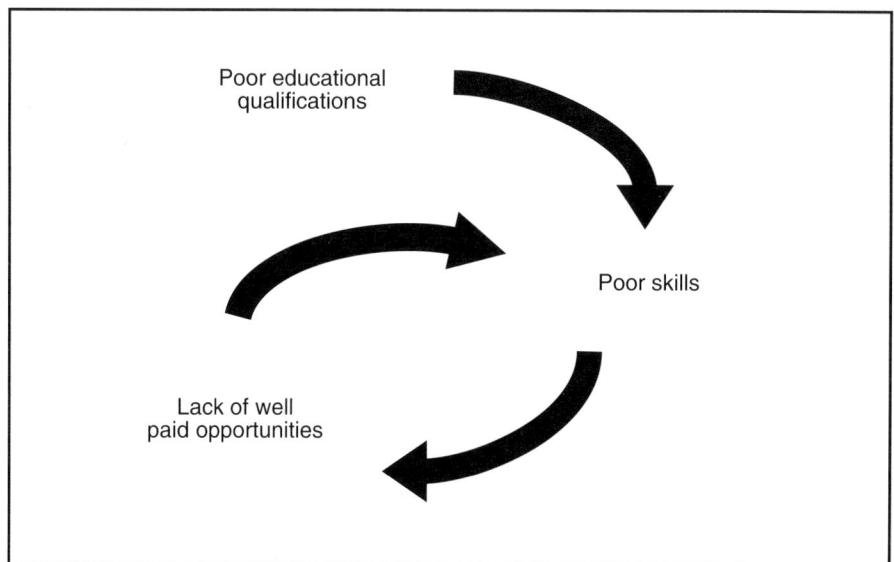

The poverty trap makes it hard for people to help themselves

The Labour Government believes in the 'root and branch' reform of the welfare state. Why?

1 It believes that spending on social security has got too high.
2 The numbers of people living in poverty have increased over the last 20 years.
3 It believes that work, rather than welfare, is the way to combat other problems e.g. crime and drugs.

To this end, the Government has embarked on a number of efforts to move people from 'welfare to work'. Each effort should not be seen in isolation. Each tackles a specific reason for not working. Before Labour came to power, many poor people were caught in the 'poverty trap'. It was simply not worth many poor people getting a job. They were better off on benefits. This is sometimes described as 'the dependency culture'. To end poverty and the dependency culture, New Labour has sought to obtain full employment. It has tried to do so by moving from welfare to work.

INVESTIGATION

Your title is **"The challenge to the welfare state"**

Your possible resources are:

◆ *Social Issues in the UK* textbook
◆ BBC Scotland video *Living on a Low Income*

Websites listed on page 43. Answer your four aims on four separate pieces of paper. The aims are:

1 To explain what the welfare state tries to do.
2 To explain the economic challenge to the welfare state.
3 To explain the social challenge to the welfare state.
4 To explain the political challenge to the welfare state.

The Labour Government has taken its inspiration and many of its ideas from policies first tried out in the USA. 'Welfare to work' is an expression borrowed from the USA. Another is the belief that the unemployed should receive a 'hand up, not a hand out'. It is a major change in thinking behind New Labour and has not been popular with some of Labour's more traditional supporters.

The New Deals

www.newdeal.gov.uk

The term 'New Deal' was first used in the USA during the depression of the 1930s. President Franklin D. Roosevelt introduced a New Deal to get people back to work. One major idea was the construction of the Interstate system across the USA. This brought work to many construction workers. They spent their earnings and paid tax, rather than claim benefits. Jobs were created in the areas of the economy where the workers spent their earnings. Unemployment in the USA decreased.

In Britain today there is a New Deal for the under 25s, a New Deal for Lone Parents and a New Deal for Partners of the Unemployed. In November 1999, Chancellor Gordon Brown also announced the New Deal for the Over 25s.

Each New Deal targets a different group of people, but the aim of each is the same: to move people from a life of depending on benefits to a life of work and independence. The New Deal believes that the unemployed have rights but also responsibilities.

Labour's New Deal for Young People gives those aged between 18 and 25 a choice of four options:

1 A job with a company which has chosen to join up for the New Deal. This guarantees wages which are higher than benefits and includes one day per week training.
2 Work with a voluntary organisation which has chosen to join up for the New Deal. Again, this includes wages higher than benefits and relevant training at college.
3 A job with the new 'Environment Taskforce'. This too includes wages and training.
4 A place at college studying full time.

According to Chancellor Gordon Brown, *"there will be no 5th option of doing nothing and being paid for it"*. Young people are allocated a New Deal adviser who tries to match up the most appropriate option for the young person. If, after a six month period, no option has been chosen, benefit is cut.

Pre-school and after-school clubs

Following precedents set in the USA, the Government has set up a range of after-school clubs in schools. Children who are entitled to free school meals now have access to a breakfast at school in the morning. Schools have also been given extra money to provide homework- and after-school clubs for pupils it feels need extra help. Some schools have set up extra summer schools and Easter revision classes.

As well as guaranteeing vulnerable young people at least two decent meals per day, there is an educational benefit to these initiatives. Those youngsters from deprived backgrounds are also those who are least likely to have facilities at home to study or do homework in a peaceful environment. They also need teacher help more than the well-off students who perhaps have professional parents who can help. Poorer children are less likely to have resources at home such as computers and access to the Internet. In some cases, it is even paper and pens that are unavailable.

For the Government, however, these clubs free up parents to work and make them less likely to remain unemployed and claim benefits. The pre- and after-school initiatives are part of the New Deal for Lone Parents.

The National Minimum Wage

The USA has had a National Minimum Wage for some time. The National Minimum Wage (NMW) came into effect in Britain in April 1999. After some negotiation between trade unions, government and employers, two rates were set for the NMW.

◆ £3.60 for those aged 21 and over. This was increased to £3.70 in 2000.
◆ £3.00 for those aged 18–20, plus those on the New Deal. This was increased to £3.20 in 2000.

The NMW has not pleased everyone. In the first place, some employers believed that they could not afford to pay the new minimum wage. They believed that it would lead to job losses. Others, such as trade unions, believed that the minimum wage was not high enough. They were unhappy too that those under 18 and those on formal apprenticeships are exempt from the minimum wage. They claimed that this group of workers was often one that needed most protection.

The working families' tax credit

See page 61.

A more personalised service

New Labour aims to target state help more effectively. Those eligible for the New Deals are assigned to a 'Gateway Advisor'. This person will try to find job and training opportunities best suited for the individual. The unemployed also have the chance to 'Dial-a-job'. The Employment Service Direct started in January 1999. Special teams are in place in job centres across the country. The unemployed can use a free phone service that puts them in touch with immediate vacancies around the country.

Responsibilities and rights

At the same time as the Government is offering new opportunities for the unemployed to find work, it has made it clear that the poor have a responsibility to take control of their lives. While the Government does not agree with the American sociologist Charles Murray (see page 52) that the poor choose to be poor, it has made the distinction between the 'deserving' and the 'undeserving poor'. As Ken Livingstone said on BBC Question Time *"I don't think anyone has a right to sit back and do nothing and expect others to pay for it. We must all put something back into society"*.

ACTIVITIES

1   Explain why New Labour wishes to change the welfare state.

Viewpoint A

"The New Deal offers the unemployed a real chance to get back to work and have a decent standard of living. It will meet the needs of all those who really want to work. There is no excuse for not signing up for one of the options".

Viewpoint B

"The New Deal is just another trendy slogan. Underneath it is the same old tried and failed training schemes. Yet again, the unemployed are being forced into taking low paid, unskilled jobs. It is a disgrace."

2   Give three differences between the two viewpoints.
3   Which view do you agree with? Give reasons for your answer.
4   Describe the benefits of the pre- and after-school clubs for
◆   pupils
◆   parents
◆   the Government.
5   What arguments are there for and against the National Minimum Wage?
6   Draw up a list of rights and responsibilities the unemployed have under New Labour.
7   Describe the efforts made by New Labour to move people from welfare to work.

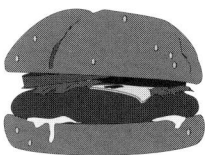

Extended writing

"New Labour is wrong to use American solutions to solve British problems." Discuss.

POVERTY IN THE UK

There is a lot of wealth in the UK. The *Sunday Times* newspaper publishes an annual Rich List. In 1999, the combined wealth of the top 1000 individuals in the UK was £114,829,000,000,000. David Beckham and his wife Victoria Adams just missed out on a place in the top 1000, as they only had a combined wealth of £20m!

The 1999 UK Top Ten Wealthy people		
1 Hans Rausing	Packaging	£3400m
2 Lord Sainsbury	Food retailing	£3100m
3 George Soros	Finance	£2000m
4 Joseph Lewis	Finance	£1750m
5 The Duke of Westminster	Land, property	£1750m
6 Lady Grantchester	Stores, mail order, football pools	£1500m
7 Garfield Weston	Food	£1500m
8 Sri and Gopi Hinduja	Finance	£1300m
9 Bruno Schroder	Banking	£1200m
10 Richard Branson	Travel, retail, entertainment	£1200m
11 Lakshmi Mittal	Steel	£1200m

Wealth is more than just money; it includes property and investments. There is no commonly agreed definition of what makes a person wealthy, rather than just comfortable. Likewise, there is no commonly agreed definition of poverty in the UK. What is poor to one person, may be quite well off to another. A Scot, struggling to get by on benefit, may be well off compared to a war refugee. We need to make the distinction between *absolute* poverty and *relative* poverty.

ABSOLUTE POVERTY

A person who lacks the very basic essentials for survival could be said to be living in absolute poverty. We associate absolute poverty today with the era before the welfare state. In absolute poverty, a person would not have a home, food and water and/or sufficient clothes.

RELATIVE POVERTY

In today's society, there are few who live in absolute poverty. By comparison with others, however, many people do live on a low income. Most people in the UK expect the basics of life. Today, the luxuries of previous generations, such as a television and video, are taken as necessities. There is clearly a distinction between existing and having a life. That can always be a matter of opinion, but a person who could not afford to go out for a meal, buy a car or go on holiday could be said to be existing, rather than living. A person could, therefore, have a job and yet still live in poverty. Despite the introduction of the National Minimum Wage, many people still have a low income.

As there is no single definition of poverty, different people disagree over what being poor is. We can however, use the statistics of the Department of Social Security (DSS) to work out approximately how many people in the UK live in poverty. The DSS compile figures on Households Below Average Income (HBAI). Those included will be persons who have an income of less than 50% of average income and/or depend on Income Support. In 1998, the average earnings (before tax) of all males was £423 per week. For all females, the figure was £307 per week. According to these figures, around one fifth of all adults live in poverty. One in three children in the UK are brought up in poverty.

Income support is a means-tested benefit, i.e. the amount a person receives depends on personal financial circumstances. Income Support is paid to people who are not in full-time work. It is different from Jobseekers Allowance (JSA). JSA is a temporary benefit, only for those who have just lost a job. After six months, the person may move on to Income Support.

ACTIVITIES

1 Explain the difference between absolute and relative poverty.
2 What is the extent of poverty in the UK?
3 Look up the DSS website www.dss.gov.uk and make a list of the different benefits that are available in the UK.

SOCIAL EXCLUSION

This is a new term which the Government uses in discussions on poverty. It is a useful term because it broadens the definition of poverty. Social exclusion is more than just the absence of money, it is the inability to take part in activities which would enable a person to get out of poverty. A student at university, for example, may be poor while studying, but could expect a well paid job on obtaining a degree. In contrast, a person who has been unemployed for some time, living solely on Income Support, may be socially excluded.

Social exclusion is:
◆ a lack of knowledge of issues in society. This could be developments in ICT or political developments or changes in the law.
◆ A powerlessness to influence change.
◆ A lack of communication

Social exclusion = poverty + wider isolation from the working community

Certain groups in society are more vulnerable to poverty than others.
◆ *Women*: as we read in Chapter One, women still tend to take more family responsibilities and are less likely than men to have a well paid job.
◆ *Lone parents*, the vast majority of whom are women.
◆ *Young people* aged 16–17 who are not entitled to benefits.
◆ *Pensioners* who are dependent on state benefits. In 1998, pensioners made up 41% of Scotland's Income Support claimants.
◆ *Rural households* with poor access to services.

- *Ethnic minorities* who have higher rates of unemployment and are more likely to have a low paid job.
- *Families on a low income with children.* Children are expensive!
- *Disabled people*: 22% of people in Scotland living on Income Support are disabled. In 1991, the figure was 7%.

The rich get rich, the poor get poorer

In 1974, a theatre group was set up in Scotland. It called itself the 7:84 Theatre company. It aimed to draw attention to the fact that 7% of the population owned 84% of the wealth. The figure has not changed much since then. A study by the *Joseph Rowntree Foundation* in 1995 found that the incomes of the richest 10% grew faster than the incomes of the bottom 10%.

THE CAUSES OF POVERTY

Just as sociologists do not all agree on the definition of poverty, there are various reasons, sometimes conflicting, on the causes of poverty.

Individual weakness

Some, such as the American Charles Murray, believe that a poverty lifestyle is an individual choice. He maintains that the welfare state has created a class in society, 'the underclass', who choose to survive on welfare benefits. According to Murray this underclass could find work, but lack the discipline and motivation to conform to the pressures of a working environment. The underclass, he maintains will sometimes work doing odd jobs, or 'homers', described as the 'black economy'. It will be involved in petty crime and/or drug dealing. Not all in the underclass will be criminals, but the welfare state, particularly for lone parents, is more attractive than working. He maintains, therefore, that poverty is an individual weakness.

Unemployment

As we read earlier in Chapter Two, Scotland has suffered the decline of its traditional industries. Rural unemployment has been a major cause of unemployment in areas such as the Scottish Borders, with the closure of the textile industries it relied upon. Even newer industries such as electronics do not offer secure long-term work. In 1998, *Viasystems* closed down its plants in Galashiels and Selkirk. Coming on top of the redundancies from *Pringle* in Hawick, the outlook for those seeking work in the Borders has become bleak. It is much harder for people living in rural communities to find work and to access services such as career advice and educational retraining.

Changing job patterns

We live in a global economy. The companies that many people now work for have operations all over the world. These multi-national companies can negotiate working conditions which suit them, rather than those of the country they are based in. In recent years there has been the growth of low paid, flexible, part-time work, sometimes described as 'McJobs'.

Government policies

Some sociologists have criticised government policy for causing poverty. Rather than progressive taxation, the Conservative Governments believed in the theory of 'trickle down' taxation. This meant that levels of direct income tax were lowered and indirect taxes such as VAT increased. The Government believed that this would give those people who were better off an incentive to work, as the Government would not be taking their earnings in tax. Wealth would 'trickle down' to the poor as more jobs were created. However, according to DSS figures, between 1979 and 1994, the richest 10% of the population saw their incomes rise by 65%. The poorest 10% saw their incomes drop by 13%.

Increases in indirect taxes hit the poor more than the rich as the poor spend proportionately more of their earnings than the rich. A 30p increase in cigarettes will affect a pensioner on Income Support more than a lawyer.

ACTIVITIES

1 Explain how each of the following can cause poverty:
◆ individual weakness
◆ unemployment
◆ changing job patterns
◆ government policies
2 "The poor only have themselves to blame."
To what extent do you agree with this view? Give reasons for your answer.

THE EFFECTS OF POVERTY

Poverty has a devastating effect on those who have to live with it.

Effect number one: housing

"We have to live in the poorest houses. Other people look down on you all the time."

"Most of the council houses have been bought. Very few change hands. Only the worst are left to rent"

Source: Life on a Low Income, 1996, SPIU, Glasgow Caledonian University

According to the pressure group *Shelter*, Scotland has the worst housing conditions in Western Europe. Its 1997 study showed that 367 000 Scottish children live in houses that are affected by dampness and condensation.

The Conservative Governments of 1979–1997 were committed to home ownership. The **1979 Sale of Council Housing Act** offered some families the opportunity to buy a quality council house at an affordable price. However, it also made it more difficult for the poorest families to secure a decent house. Only the best quality houses in the best council neighbourhoods were bought. This left a smaller pool of less desirable houses available for those who could not obtain a mortgage. In addition, local councils were not allowed to spend the money they received from the sale of council houses on upgrading the ones that were not sold.

The number of private houses being built has increased from 73% of all new houses in 1983 to 82.6% in 1994. By contrast, only 3.1% of new houses built were in the public sector. It is very difficult for those on a low income to obtain a mortgage. Good, affordable, rented accommodation is also difficult to find. The unemployed are twice as likely to live in a damp house than those in work. This problem is made worse because the unemployed are more likely to spend a lot of time at home. This leads to higher heating costs. It also leads to emotional problems such as depression, stress and anxiety.

Effect number two: education

In 1999, the Scottish Teachers union the EIS, published details of research it had carried out on the effect of poor housing on education. It found that pupils from poor housing did less well at school. Children from better off families had a much higher chance of gaining three Highers or more and going on to university. 83% of children from affluent backgrounds go on to higher education, while only 11% of young people from deprived backgrounds do. Children from poorer families were also much more likely to get into trouble at school and be excluded. Other research from the Joseph Rowntree Foundation showed that many lone parents deprived themselves of food to feed their children.

Effect number three: bad health

A 1999 study by the National Office for Statistics showed a huge gulf in survival rates between rich and poor victims of cancer. The research showed that thousands of lives could be saved if the poor had the same chances of survival as the well off. For 14 types of cancer, including major killers such as lung, bowel and breast cancer, the most affluent had a 16% higher chance of surviving another five years than the most deprived. The better off also had a 5% better chance of surviving seven other important cancers such as cervical, prostate and ovarian. During the period of the study, 1986–1990, a total of 12 745 deaths could have been avoided. Poorer resistance to disease and lack of awareness and access to care were described by doctors as the reasons.

Effect number four: debt

The vast majority of enquiries to the Citizens Advice Bureau come from families who have run into debt. These debts are more likely to be arrears in rent, mortgage, gas, electricity and Council Tax than the credit card debts incurred by better off debtors. These types of debts are punished more harshly in terms of repossession, fines and disconnection. Low-income families with children feel the pressure to get into debt all the greater.

Low-income families also have less chance of using credit. The points system used by banks and credit card companies means that low-income families are more likely to be refused low interest credit. A well off customer may even be able to obtain a discount by paying with ready cash. Shops such as *Crazy George* offer credit for consumer goods at low weekly repayments. Over the course of a year, however, these repayments can mount up.

INVESTIGATION

Your title is "The effects of poverty on children"

Your possible resources are:

- *Social Issues in the UK* textbook
- BBC Scotland video *Gender and Race: Society*
- BBC Scotland audio tape *Inequalities in Health Care*
- Scottish Poverty Information Unit: http://spiu.gcal.ac.uk
- Joseph Rowntree Foundation: www.jrf.org.uk

You should answer each of the following questions on a separate piece of paper.

1 What are the effects of poverty on housing?
2 What are the effects of poverty on education?
3 What are the effects of poverty on health?
4 What are the effects of poverty on the break up of families?

You should try to sum up your findings in a balanced conclusion on a final piece of paper.

The unemployed are also at the mercy of unscrupulous 'loan sharks' who will lend ready cash but charge extortionate rates of interest – and worse if the money is not repaid.

Effect number four: impact on family life
"Sometimes they say: Look at the horrible clothes he's got on. I'm not playing with you, you look horrible!"

Source: Joseph Rowntree Enquiry

In these label conscious days, children feel a stigma at coming from a low-income family. Parents and schools may try to stop teasing and bullying, but this is not always possible. Financial difficulties may make people lose contact with friends. Families are more likely to argue when money is tight. Marital break-up is more common among families living in poverty.

NEW LABOUR'S ATTACKS ON POVERTY

"Poverty in Scotland casts a shadow over the new century. It is the single biggest issue for the parliament to address."

Ms Gill Scott, Scottish Poverty Information Unit

New Labour has agreed with the sociologist Gill Scott that ending poverty should be a major priority for the Government. At the 1999 Labour Party conference, Tony Blair set Labour the goal of ending child poverty by 2003. To do this it has placed 'social exclusion' at the top of its priorities.

The Government has set up a new Social Exclusion Unit in London to examine solutions to poverty and other social issues in the UK. Social Security changes have been put in place which we shall examine. Social Security remains a UK power, and the Scottish Parliament does not have control over Social Security changes. The Scottish Parliament can, however, take action and it has set up a special parliamentary committee, the Social Inclusion, Housing and Voluntary Sector committee.

The Labour Government has declared that tackling poverty is not just the responsibility of government. It believes in a 'joined-up' approach in which local authorities, voluntary groups and private sector organisations all have a role to play in tackling the causes and effects of poverty and social exclusion. Individuals also have their part to play. The Government is clear that people living in poverty have rights, but they have responsibilities too. The Government recognises the effect that poverty has on other vital issues such as housing, education, health and crime.

THE SOCIAL INCLUSION AGENDA

Social *Exclusion*
"A new-born baby returns with his mother to a bed and breakfast

that is cold, damp, cramped. A mother who has no job, no family to support her ... a father nowhere to be seen. For this child, individual potential hangs by a thread."

Social *Inclusion*

"A second baby, in the same maternity ward returns to a prosperous home ... and a father with a decent income and an even larger sense of pride. Expectations are sky high."

Tony Blair, Labour Party Conference, 1999

Social exclusion means poverty. It is more than a lack of money, it is a lack of hope and a lack of expectation. It is also a lack of will and ability to get out of poverty. **Social inclusion,** on the other hand, means security. It means high hopes and expectations. It means the ability to choose informed options in life. It means being an active citizen.

"We must create a climate in which good health can flourish."
Sam Galbraith

www.hebs.scot.nhs.uk

In 1999, the Scottish Executive set itself a 10-point target to promote social inclusion and end poverty. It hopes that by the year 2020 it will have achieved all of its aims.

The 10-point plan

1 End child poverty.
2 Improve education for all primary school pupils, so that all can read, write and count to the best of their ability on entering secondary school.
3 Ensure that all pupils leave secondary school with the maximum skills and qualifications possible.
4 Ensure that all 19-year-olds are in education, training or work.
5 Ensure full employment in Scotland.
6 Ensure that everyone is involved in learning new skills or knowledge.
7 Make all elderly people financially secure.
8 Increase the number of healthy, active older people.
9 Reduce inequalities between different parts of the country.
10 Increase neighbours' satisfaction with their housing and community.

Certain parts of the plan are already up and running. The Scottish Executive has set up a network of Healthy Living Centres in Scotland's most deprived communities. These centres try to help people stop smoking and reduce alcohol intake. The money has come from the National Lottery 'sixth good cause' announced in 1997. The Government believes, however, that merely informing

Darnley before the launch of the Glen Oaks Housing Association ...

... and after

Tommy Sheridan MSP backs the new Housing Association homes in Pollock

people of the effect of an unhealthy lifestyle is not enough. People must have an incentive to adopt a healthy lifestyle. Poor housing, unemployment and bad environment are seen as the root cause of ill health.

HOUSING

The Government has set up New Housing Partnerships between tenants, local councils and the private sector to improve the quality of rented housing. Central to this is a move away from the old fashioned landlord/tenant relationship of old style council housing. Under this system, the landlord, who was the local authority, maintained houses from a distance. There was little input from the tenants on the design of the buildings. Tenants therefore had little incentive to improve the local area. If anything needed improving it was 'the council's problem'. There was little sense of ownership or control over the quality of housing or its environment.

In recent years, a new type of public/private partnership has created a new type of housing. The Glen Oaks Housing Association in Darnley, Glasgow, is a stunning example of the changes that can be made. Darnley used to be a byword for all the evils of a deprived housing estate. The housing was frequently cold and damp. The architecture was grim and purpose-built for graffiti artists and vandals. Crime and drug taking was rife. Darnley was not a pleasant place to live.

Tenants voted to set up a housing association, Glen Oaks, which would own and control housing. Tenants could join Glen Oaks for as little as £1. In a housing association, the elected committee, all of whom live in the area, make all the decisions about rents, repairs, developments and who is entitled to live in the area. There is a combination of private and rented accommodation. There is the opportunity to part-buy, part-rent homes at an affordable price. This means that those who are in a low paid or insecure job can have the chance to buy part of a home. Those who have a housing association home must sign a 'Good Neighbour' contract. This gives tenants the responsibility to maintain properties and not be anti-social towards their neighbours. The committee has the power to evict anti-social tenants. Residents say that the Glen Oaks accommodation is so good, it is difficult to tell which houses are privately owned.

In 1999, Glen Oaks expanded into the Pollock area of Glasgow. A £2.6 million housing project of high-quality homes replaced the previous local authority-controlled houses which were poorly insulated and built. This time, the local people played a key part in the planning and design of the new homes. According to local MSP Tommy Sheridan, the homes are a *"tribute to the residents of North Pollock and Glen Oaks Housing Association"*.

ACTIVITIES

1 Explain the difference between social exclusion and social inclusion.

2 Match up the following to either social *exclusion* or social *inclusion*:
Drugs – good job – voting – going out for a meal – bad housing – unemployment – playing sport – a balanced diet – abusing alcohol – doing well at school – joining a political party – writing a letter to a newspaper – depression – doing DIY around the home – school homework club – truanting from school – trouble with the police – saving for Christmas presents – going on holiday – lying in bed all day

3 Copy the 10-point plan into your notes. Do you feel the 10-point plan is too ambitious/impossible or vague? Give reasons for your answer.

4 Are there other priorities you could add to your plan? Which aspects of social exclusion do you think are the most important to tackle? Give reasons for your answer.

5 Design your 'ideal home'.

6 Would you rather rent or buy your ideal home? Give reasons for your answer.

7 What differences have Glen Oaks Housing Association made to housing in Darnley and Pollock?

8 What are the advantages housing association homes have over 'traditional' council housing?

The Government has pledged funds to provide additional support for housing associations. It has also started the Empty Homes Initiative to bring empty properties back into use to prevent homelessness. The Rough Sleepers Initiative has set itself the target of eliminating overnight rough sleeping by the end of the first term of the Scottish Parliament. Housing pressure groups such as Shelter have tried to persuade the Government that the aim should be to stop people becoming homeless in the first place.

www.shelter.org.uk

LONE PARENTS

Why is there a fuss over lone parents? Part of the reason for this is their growing numbers. Increasing numbers of children are now born outside of marriage and are being brought up in lone parent families. The main reasons for this are the decline in numbers of people getting married and higher divorce rates.

CASE STUDY

Lone parents

British society has had a conflicting view over women and their relationship with work. Until recently, the male of the family was seen as the 'breadwinner'. As such, women with children who went out to work, were seen as 'bad mothers'. On the other hand, women who stay at home to look after children are not valued. This is the 'damned if you do, damned if you don't' scenario. According to one woman, *"you are made to feel a second-class citizen if you stay at home. If you fill in a form and you say 'housewife', you feel like you are brain dead. We need support to get the balance right."*

In the last few years, unmarried women with children who do not work have been branded as 'spongers'. Lone parents have been the subject of a great deal of attention, most of it negative. Lone parents have been stereotyped as careless and carefree women who have no desire to make a contribution to society, yet are prepared to claim the social security benefits which are provided for the unemployed who have responsibility for a child.

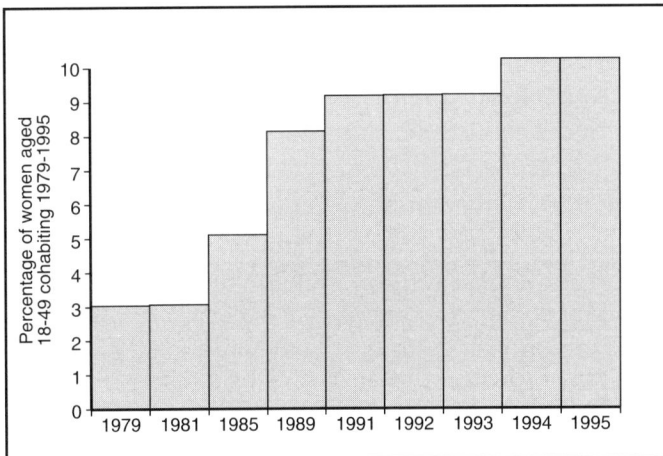

Source 1

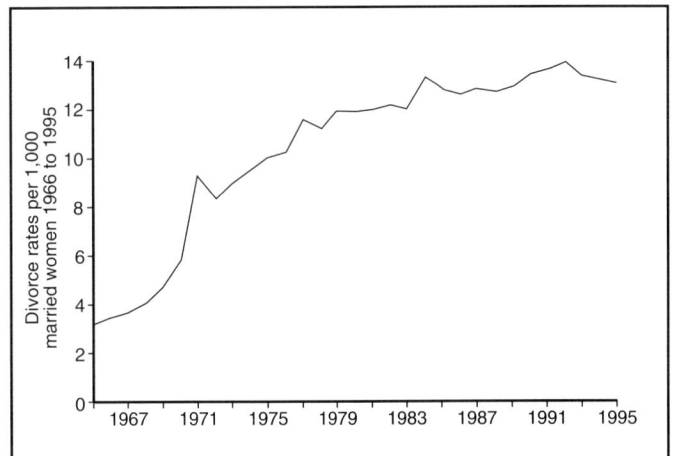

Source 2

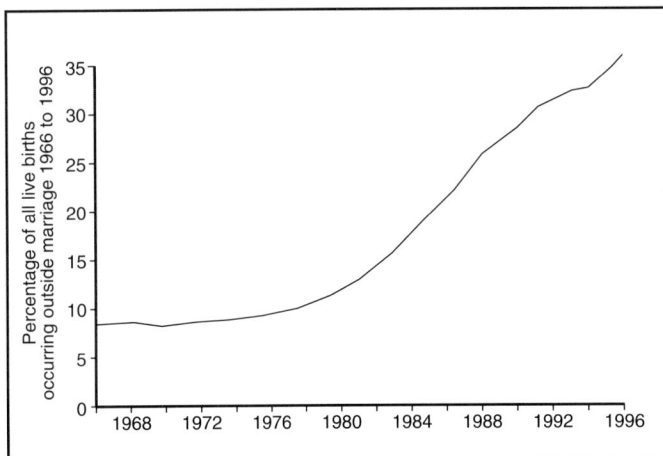

Source 3
(Source: DSS, 1999)

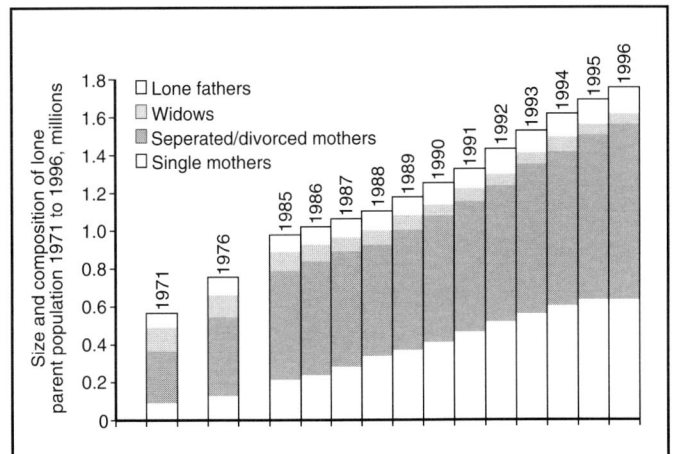

Source 4

Using Sources 1, 2, 3 and 4, answer the following questions.

1 What evidence is there that more people have been co-habiting (living together outside of marriage)?

2 What evidence is there that more people are getting divorced?

3 *"There are more unmarried mothers than ever before."*
What evidence is there to support the above statement?

4 *"There are just as many lone fathers as lone mothers. Most lone mothers have been married and got divorced."* What evidence is there **for** and **against** the above statement?

It is estimated that around a quarter of the next generation of children will spend some time in a lone-parent household. It is untrue to say that parents in these households do not want to work. The Government reports that over 80% of lone parents want some kind of work and do not like being at home all day looking after children. They want work, but face problems over a lack of advice and proper child-care arrangements. Some lone parents balance very high powered careers with the responsibility of looking after children. In 1998 Carly Fiorina, a lone parent, became head of computer giant Hewlett–Packard. Joanne Rowling, author of the famous Harry Potter children's novels, is another successful single mum.

Divorcee Ann Budge is a partner in Newel and Budge, a computer software consultancy in Edinburgh. It has an annual turnover of £16 million and profits of around £1.4 million. When Ann set up the business in 1985 she was a single parent with a twelve-year-old daughter. Her daughter Carol, now 26, works in the business. "*I find myself getting irritated by the stereotyping of single parents because we are all different, as different as any man or woman in terms of income, careers, abilities and circumstances. Single parents probably have more reason to be driven than anyone else, so what's the big surprise?*"

While not *all* lone parents are poor, many are. Around 60% of lone parents have less than half the average income. In September 1999, five out of six lone parents claimed a means-tested benefit such as Income Support. Less than one third of lone parents own their own home, compared with three quarters of married couples. This has severe effects for the children in lone-parent families. Poor children are much more likely to go without expensive fashion items than other children. Children can often be cruel to other children who they perceive as being poor. Bullying, being called cruel names and being left out of activities, are common experiences of children from poor families.

It is therefore difficult to see why women would choose to have this kind of lifestyle. One of the problems facing lone parents was the 'poverty trap'. A person was poor living on benefits, but because the type of job available was likely to be low paid, the benefits lost

Ann and Carol Budge at work

by going out to work meant that there was no financial incentive to get a job. The result was unhappiness for the lone parent and child, and a loss of income for the Government.

ACTIVITY

Extended writing

"Stereotypes of lone parents are unfair, however lone parents do have more chance of being poor than other households."

Discuss this statement.

Lone parent Carol Ann Gemmill from Rutherglen, Glasgow. Ms Gemmill is attending a drama course as part of the New Deal for Lone Parents.

What has the Government done to help lone parents?

In 1998, the Government launched the New Deal for Lone Parents. The New Deal was launched as a voluntary initiative for lone parents. Its aim was to get lone parents back to work. The New Deal borrowed much of its ideas from the American experience, especially the scheme in the state of Wisconsin. Wisconsin operates a more compulsory policy, usually described as 'tough love'. In Wisconsin, lone parents who do not accept a job receive no benefits at all. Some people believe that the Wisconsin scheme will eventually come into place in the UK.

All lone parents on Income Support with children over five years and three months are contacted by the Benefits Agency. Other parents can contact the Benefits Agency earlier if they wish. The lone parent will be given an appointment with a Personal Advisor who will attempt to demonstrate how the parent will be better off at work. Advice will be given on identifying training and job opportunities and interviewing skills.

The Working Families Tax Credit

A key part of welfare to work is the Working Families Tax Credit which was introduced in October 1999. It is not aimed solely at lone parents; married couples or those co-habiting can apply as well (provided one person is working already). It is not a benefit. Instead, when a lone parent finds work, less tax is paid. It is organised by the Inland Revenue rather than the Benefits Agency. Employers are instructed to pay eligible staff 'tax credits' by putting them under a different tax code. From April 2000 it went straight into pay packets. It is hoped that this will avoid people being embarrassed when claiming the benefit. The tax credit lasts for 26 weeks. Once this period is up, the person can reapply.

Parents are eligible if:

◆ they have savings of less than £8000
◆ one or both work more than 16 hours per week
◆ they have one or more children under the age of 16 at home (under 19 if in full-time education).

Individual payments depend on circumstances and pay levels. However, in October 1999, the Government guaranteed a minimum income of £200 a week for a family with a full-time worker. The minimum for a part-time worker doing at least 16 hours would be £145 per week.

The Government also helps with child-care costs. This is up to 70% of costs up to £100 per week for one child and £150 for two or more children. The Government estimates that around 1.3 million low income families with children are better off under the Working

Parents Tax Credit. Chancellor Gordon Brown claims that 800 000 children living in poverty benefit.

The Tax Credit has met with some criticism, however. The first is that the rules exclude those who work under 16 hours per week for one employer. Some part-time workers will have two part-time jobs. They may work more than 16 hours per week, but for two different employers and therefore are ineligible for the tax credit. Others have suggested that unfair employers will take advantage of the scheme. They may pay only the National Minimum Wage of £3.60 per hour, knowing that the Government (or rather the taxpayer) will top up the workers' pay packet through the tax credit.

www.inlandrevenue.gov.uk

ACTIVITIES

1 What are the stereotypes of lone parents?
2 Why are these stereotypes inaccurate?
3 What differences are there between 'tough love' in Wisconsin and New Labour's New Deal for Lone Parents?
4 Describe how the Working Families Tax Credit works.
5 What are some of the criticisms of the tax credit?

HEALTH CARE IN THE UK

THE NATIONAL HEALTH SERVICE

The National Health Service (NHS) has widely been seen to be the 'jewel in the crown' of the welfare state. While the Conservative Governments of 1979–1997 challenged many of the assumptions of the welfare state, it did not abolish the NHS.

The NHS today has undergone many changes, but its key aims remains intact:

1 To promote good health and to avoid bad health. Prevention is better than cure.
2 To provide a health service which is free to everyone at the point of use, regardless of their financial background, age, race or religion.

The NHS is more than just hospitals. It includes doctors who are General Practitioners (GPs), dentists, chiropodists, speech therapists, community health services and mental health services.

There is no doubt that Scots have better health now than in 1948 when the NHS was set up. The average life expectancy of men today is 72 years; in 1948, it was 63. The average life expectancy of a woman is 77; in 1948, it was 72. Throughout the UK, the NHS employs around one million people. On a typical day, almost 700 000 people visit their family NHS doctor and 130 000 visit a NHS dentist. District nurses will make 100 000 visits and ambulances will make 8000 emergency journeys. NHS surgeons will perform around 220 hip operations, 750 heart operations and 2100 kidney operations. All this costs a lot of money. Around £3.6 billion is spent on health, which is about one third of the Scottish Parliament's entire budget.

It is a political decision to have a NHS. Not every country has one. In the USA, for example, patients have to pay directly for treatment to the hospital. Patients can have Private Medical

Insurance (PMI) or be fortunate to have an employer who will provide an occupational health plan. If you do not have money to pay, you will receive state help, which is run by volunteer medical staff and is of vastly inferior quality. Most British people would not like to see this form of health care in Britain or return to the days before the NHS.

Yet, despite the support and loyalty of the public towards the NHS, it always seems to be in crisis.

ACTIVITIES

1   What are the main aims of the National Health Service?
2   Why is prevention better than cure?
3   Why is the NHS more than just hospitals and doctors?
4   What evidence is there that health in the UK has improved since the NHS was created?

How satisfied would you say you are with the running of the National Health Service?

	1983	1991	1996
satisfied	55%	40%	36%
neither satisfied/dissatisfied	20%	19%	14%
dissatisfied	25%	41%	50%

"The public are increasingly unhappy about the way the NHS is run."
(Source: British Social Attitudes Report, 1997)
5   Give **two** pieces of evidence to support the above statement.

The public have been increasingly unhappy about the way the NHS is run. Each year brings new scare stories of hospital waiting lists and shortages of nurses and beds. Why is this the case?

Increased demand

The pioneers of the NHS believed that as the NHS improved health care, people would make less demands on health. This has not been the case. On the contrary, as people are living longer, more demands are made on the resources of the NHS.

New technology

Medical science has come a long way since 1948. Among the list of routine operations that did not exist in 1948 are
◆ heart by-passes
◆ heart transplants
◆ open brain surgery
◆ keyhole surgery
◆ hip replacement

These operations cost money.

New diseases

While the old diseases such as rickets, smallpox and cholera have been wiped out, new diseases such as HIV/AIDS, hepatitis and *E. coli* poisoning have appeared. These diseases cost the NHS a great deal of money.

Increased expectations

The British public today expect to be cured when ill. Before the NHS, most ordinary people were ignorant about medical science and their rights in a medical situation. Today, the availability and advance of medical science has brought increased expectations by the public. The Major Conservative Government introduced the **Patients' Charter**, which spelt out the maximum waiting times for operations and the high standards of care to be delivered. It gave patients the choice over doctors and hospitals. These developments have increased the financial stress on the NHS and increased pressures on medical staff.

ACTIVITY

Draw a spider diagram which explains the new demands on the NHS.

THE PRIVATE ALTERNATIVE

Just as some parents who do not wish to send their children to state education have the right to choose private education, taxpayers who do not wish state health care have the right to choose private health care.

Private health care in the UK is not new. In fact, in the days before the NHS, nearly all health care was dependent on the ability to pay. The only alternative to the private sector was the voluntary hospitals, run by charity organisations.

Today, many patients who opt out of NHS care still have to pay National Insurance contributions and Income Tax. They have therefore chosen to pay twice for their health care. Most private patients pay for their treatment through a form of Private Medical Insurance (PMI). This is offered by companies such as *BUPA* and *AXA*. PMI works on the same principle as car or home insurance. The lower the possibility that you will claim (and actually use the service), the lower the payments, or premiums. The greater the chance that you will claim on the service, in this case the greater chance you have of being ill, the higher the premium. The number who have taken this option has grown in recent years. In the 1950s, only around 2% of the population were covered by PMI. In 1998, this figure had grown to 12.7%.

Why?

1 The main reason was due to a loss in confidence in the NHS. The biggest growth in PMI came during the 1980s when there was a lot of reorganisation going on within the NHS. Scare stories in the press, allied to real evidence of long waiting lists, led many people to consider going private.

2 During the 1980s those in work became richer. The relative cost of PMI decreased as incomes grew. PMI (for healthy patients!) can cost less per day than a packet of cigarettes.

3 Many companies began to offer PMI, along with the company car and cheap loans, as a 'perk' to attract key skilled workers. PMI has the advantage for large companies in that it enables skilled workers who need routine operations to be in and out of hospital (and back to work) quickly. There are not many top footballers who have their injuries operated on in a NHS hospital!

PMI FOR AND AGAINST

Opinion is divided on the benefits of PMI. A generation of people have now taken the NHS for granted, and are familiar with long waiting times for operations. Feelings for and against PMI are not so strong. Until recently, the Labour Party was strongly opposed to PMI, but now believe that the private sector can work alongside the NHS.

For PMI

1 It is an individual's right to spend their money in the way they choose. If the individual wants to spend it on health care, rather than beer, that is a choice anyone should have in a democratic country.

2 PMI *helps* the NHS. It takes away people who otherwise would be on NHS waiting lists and treats them in the private sector. The NHS, therefore, is there for people who really need it.

3 With shorter waiting lists, less taxes need to be spent on health care and can be spent on other government priorities e.g. education.

4 Without the high salaries paid in the private sector, talented doctors and other medical staff would leave the country to go to the USA. Some doctors work in both private and NHS hospitals, so the private sector is helping the NHS.

Against PMI

1 It is immoral that money can buy health. It is argued that health is not a consumer good, like beer. All human life should be equally important, regardless of wealth.

2 PMI *weakens* the NHS. It poaches the top doctors and medical staff away from the NHS with the lure of higher salaries and an easier job. The NHS would be a higher quality organisation if there were no private sector stealing the staff the NHS has trained.

3 PMI is only interested in healthy people! It specialises in cosmetic and short-stay operations. If you have a serious or life-threatening condition, PMI would be too expensive for most people. The NHS has improved the lives of millions. More money should be invested in it to bring it back to international standard.

4 PMI relies on the NHS to keep its insurance premiums down. If the NHS was not there to treat the old and the seriously ill, PMI premiums would be much dearer and fewer people would take out insurance.

DEBATE

"The individual should have the right to buy the best health care that they can afford."

Susan Deacon, Scotland's first ever Minister for Health and Community Care

SCOTTISH HEALTH CARE SOLUTIONS

The National Health Service is a UK-wide organisation. Until 1999, health care policy was decided by the UK Government in London. It did take into account the specific health needs of different areas of the country. For example, the Scottish Office, based in Edinburgh, took responsibility for meeting the health needs of Scotland.

Since the creation of the Scottish Parliament, in 1999, however, health has become a *devolved* power. This means that new laws regarding health can be made in Scotland, and will only apply to Scotland.

The New Labour Government elected in 1997 set out its priorities for Scotland in two important publications.

1 *Towards a Healthier Scotland*
2 *Designed to Care*

The new Scottish executive set up a Ministry and parliamentary committee for Health and Community Care. Its first ever Minister was Susan Deacon.

Responsibility for meeting these needs rests with a 'mixed economy'. This is composed of government, the private sector, the voluntary sector and the individual looking after their own health.

TOWARDS A HEALTHIER SCOTLAND

"We cannot have a health service which only concentrates on sickness – we have to promote health as well".

June Andrews, Scottish Secretary, Royal College of Nursing

Scotland is often referred to as the 'sick man of Europe'. Only in Scotland can you buy a 'Mars bar supper'! Scotland suffers from higher rates of cancer from smoking and coronary heart disease due to poor diet and inactivity.

Towards a Healthier Scotland puts the reduction of cancer and heart disease at the top of its priorities. It also aims this drive at Scotland's one million children and young people. As well as treating the symptoms of ill health, for the first time ever the Government has recognised the connection between ill health and poverty, unemployment, bad housing and poor education.

The Government believes that its wider attacks on 'social exclusion', such as the welfare to work programme, new community schools, childcare centres and housing partnerships, will promote good health. According to Sam Galbraith (who was a brain surgeon before entering politics) *"These initiatives will change 21st century Scotland for the better – just as the measures to improve public sanitation did at the turn of the 20th century".*

The Health of the Nation, 1998

Population (est)	5 120 000	(2021) 4 993 000
Life expectancy	male 72.6 years	female 78.1 years
Survival rates from breast cancer	(1988) 66.3%	(1998) 74.5%
Teenage pregnancies	8.7 per 1000	
No natural teeth	(1972) 44% of all adults	(1995) 17% of all adults

Tackling cancer

Around 30 000 new cases of cancer are recorded every year in Scotland. One in three Scots will develop the disease and one in four will die from it. Tobacco smoking is the most preventable cause of ill health and early death in Scotland. Smoking is responsible for one in five of all deaths in Scotland.

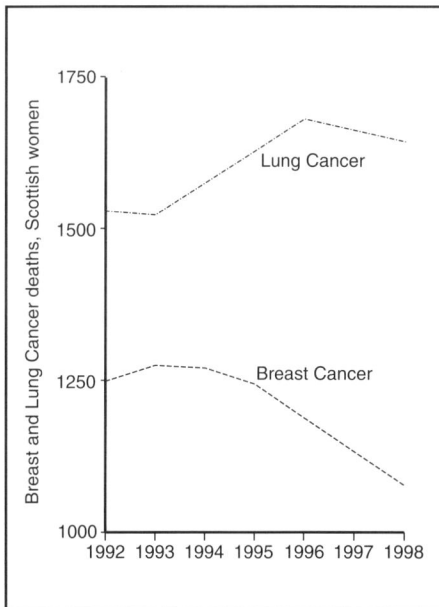

Deaths from lung and breast cancer among women in Scotland

ACTIVITIES

1 Why can Scotland be described as the 'sick man of Europe'?
2 Do you eat a healthy diet? Draw up a typical diary of your weekly diet. Award yourself:
- 5 points for a 'sin' of chocolate biscuits and/or bar of chocolate
- 10 points for a fish supper
- 10 points for a curry/kebab/pizza
  Deduct:
- 5 points for fruit
- 5 points for fresh vegetables
- 10 points for pasta meal or salad
- 10 points for a sporting activity over 40 mins

Every year the NHS spends £140m on treating smoking related illnesses. In August 1999, Sir David Carter, Scotland's Chief Medical Officer, warned that we are losing the battle over the increase in smoking among young women, *"You just have to walk the streets to see the truth".* He called for an increase in bans on smoking in public places. However, prohibition on its own has a limited value. More and better smoking education is also required in schools. Just saying 'don't do it' does not work. Instead, young people should be more aware of the consequences if they choose to smoke. As Sir David Carter himself concludes, *"at the end of the day we all determine our own destiny".*

Smokers take more sick leave than non-smokers, costing Scottish industry over £33 million a year. Smoking rates for children, especially girls, are a particular cause for concern. Research shows that almost two thirds of smokers themselves want to stop and one third of smokers support restrictions on smoking in public places.

The Scottish Executive has set targets for cutting smoking, the main cause of lung cancer. It aims to reduce the number of 12–15 year olds who smoke from 14% to 11%. Ultimately, it is hoped to drive the figure down even further. Another target is to reduce the number of women who smoke during pregnancy from 29% to 20%. The government already has invested over £5 million in health education and advertising campaigns. The aim is to counter the tactics of the tobacco companies who market smoking as sophisticated and who target young people. The companies need to do this as smoking has killed off one fifth of their previous customers! The Executive is trying to make smoking 'uncool' and anti-social. New laws already ban tobacco advertising in sport. New 'stop smoking' clinics have been set up and free nicotine replacement therapy is available to the less well off, who tend to smoke the most.

The Executive has set up a major advertising campaign to encourage the early screening of breast cancer among women and testicular cancer among men.

ACTIVITIES

Extended writing

"Smoking should be banned in all public places."
Do you agree or not?
Contact:
www.hebs.scot.nhs.uk
www.ash.org.uk
http://forest-on-smoking.org.uk

Ally McCoist

Coronary heart disease

Early deaths and illnesses from coronary heart disease and strokes are also a priority. Major contributory causes are smoking, poor diet and lack of physical activity. Research has shown that

- 91% of British schoolchildren aged 7–11 are driven to school. In 1971, the figure was 20%.
- 31% of boys and 33% of girls aged 11–15 watch television for 4 or more hours per week.
- 23% of boys and 4% of girls aged 11–15 play computer games for more than 4 hours per week.

Again, a huge health promotional drive, including the use of sporting personalities, has been used to get people to 'Save a Life – Your Own'. Former Scottish rugby captain Gavin Hastings was used in a famous advert encouraging people to take regular walks. Ally McCoist, the famous Scottish footballer and pundit has also helped with the campaign:

"You don't have to work out in a gym every day to keep fit and healthy. Take it easy. Walk down to the shops. If you take a bus to work, get off a stop earlier and walk the rest. Eat what you like, but enjoy everything in moderation. I make sure that I eat a good, balanced diet during the week – and I enjoy a pie at half-time"

1 Why do you think the Government uses celebrities such as Gavin Hastings and Ally McCoist in its health promotion campaigns?

2 *"Health promotion campaigns are effective."* Give reasons for and against this point of view. Overall, which point of view do you agree with?

"Being poor has a devastating effect on your health."

1 What evidence is there in Source I to support this point of view?

2 Give two differences between Source I and Source 2 on healthy living between well off and poor parts of town.

REDUCE HEALTH INEQUALITIES

When the NHS was set up it aimed to treat everyone in the country equally, regardless of income. While the NHS continues to treat people for free at the point of need, there has been a growing gap between the health of the comfortably off and the health of the poor. In 1979 the *Black Report* was published. It showed that the poor were dying before the rich and that there were huge differences between rich and poor in illnesses such as cancer, heart disease and strokes. The Conservative Government ignored the report and maintained that health inequalities were due to 'bad' lifestyle choices.

Source 1

In 1994, Greater Glasgow Health Board compared standards of health in Bearsden, a wealthy suburb of Glasgow, and neighbouring Drumchapel, a poor housing estate. A baby born in Drumchapel can expect to die 10 years before a baby born in Bearsden. Drumchapel is one mile from Bearsden.

A Scottish Office study in 1998, *Deprivation and Health in Scotland*, showed that people under 65 in the poorest areas are almost twice as likely to have a heart attack. Poor men are also less likely to recover from operations and more likely to require further surgery. It found that those in poor areas were more likely to get cancer, have strokes and commit suicide.

Source 2

By contrast, those whose postcodes lay in the better off parts of town, as well as having better health, had better health facilities. There were more doctors and dentists and shorter waiting lists. Breast cancer was as common for better off women, but early detection rates were higher and therefore fewer more affluent women died from the disease.

The Wealth of the Nation survey by market research firm CACI in 1999 revealed the vast gap in earnings between different groups of people in Scotland. For example, 24.3% of households in Murrayfield in Edinburgh (EH12) earned over £50,000 per year. By contrast, 74.2% of households in Bridgeton, Glasgow earned less than £13,000 per year. It costs a minimum of £300,000 for a sandstone terraced house in Murrayfield. A two bedroom flat in Bridgeton would cost less than £40,000.

DEAD POOR — WHY?

There are a number of explanations, many of which are linked.

Long-term unemployment

This is the main reason for poverty. Poverty in Scotland today tends to be concentrated. In Greater Glasgow, more than half of all children live in a deprived housing estate. Across Scotland the figure is one in five. There are parts of town where unemployment is as high as 85% of the adult population. Living on a low income means a lot of stress worrying about how to pay bills or look after children. There is little scope for luxuries. The unemployed tend to have a poor diet. The poor are doubly punished for living in a poor area.

Firstly, large supermarkets, with lower prices, tend to be based in out-of-town areas, where shoppers arrive by car and buy large quantities. Better off people, by earning a monthly salary, can afford to take advantage of these discounts in food. Secondly, these large supermarkets will also have a range of fresh, healthy foods.

These facilities are often not available in poor areas. Only small quantities of food can be afforded at a time. There is a lack of choice in shops. Lack of competition means the shop owner can charge higher prices. Prices are higher in the first place because a small shop-owner cannot buy in bulk to make savings in the way big supermarkets can.

The selection of foods available in local shops is less too. The shop owner cannot risk stocking fresh fruits and vegetables which may not sell. Pies, sausages and tinned or frozen foods are much less healthy, but more affordable for those on a low income.

Stress

Living in a poor area can mean emotional problems, which in turn lead to physical ill-health. A lack of money and worries over debt can lead to people escaping by smoking, over drinking or taking drugs. When the individual sees no hope for the future in getting work and out of poverty, it is very tempting to choose a lifestyle that brings immediate release but long-term pain.

Poor housing

Many houses in poor areas were badly built and ill thought out. Dampness is a common problem. In others it is the isolation and lack of social and recreational facilities. Vandalism and crime are serious problems in badly-designed housing. These factors lead to emotional and physical ill-health.

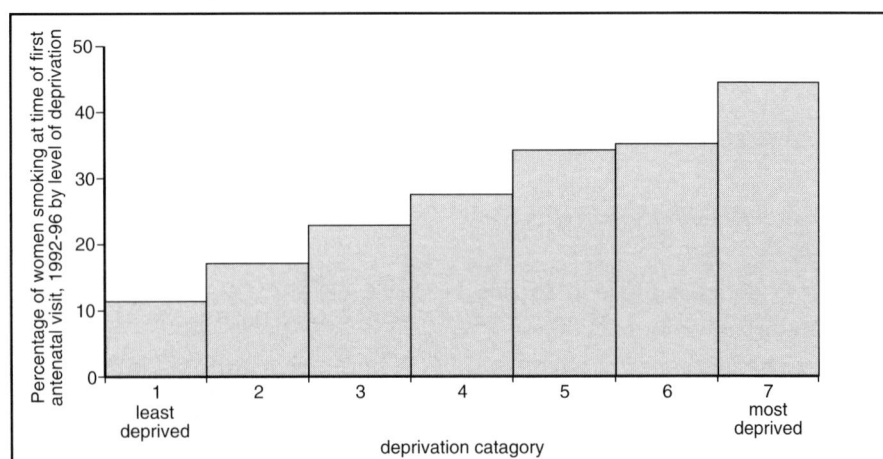

The link between smoking habits and deprivation amongst pregnant women

The Scottish Executive has recognised the links between 'social exclusion' and ill health. Its health priorities are aimed not just at treating the symptoms of ill-health, but the underlying causes. While educating people to take personal responsibility for their health, the Government's 'social inclusion' agenda aims to improve standards of living which in turn will lead to better health.

ACTIVITIES

1   Draw a spider diagram which explains the link between poverty and ill-health.

Viewpoint A

"Poverty cannot be used as an excuse for bad health. Fruit and vegetables are just as cheap as junk food. Cigarettes and alcohol are even more expensive. Sports such as running are cheap, healthy and morale boosting. No-one forces anyone to have a bad diet. With will-power, determination and some self-pride, it is perfectly possible to live a healthy life on a low income".

Viewpoint B

"The link between living on a low income is as clear as day. Those who lecture the poor on their bad diet should try living on £30 per week. There are few shops in poor areas that stock cheap, fresh food. The constant stress of living in a depressing area and trying to feed children on a budget would make anyone reach for some comfort food – or drink".

2   What are the differences between the two viewpoints on the link between poverty and bad health?
3   Which view do you agree with most? Give reasons for your answer.
4   Watch the BBC video *Gender and Race: Society*. Describe actions that have been taken to improve diets in Wester Hailes, Edinburgh.

Designed to care

The Government revealed its proposals for the changes to Scotland's health service in its white paper, *Designed to Care*. Many of these changes came into place in April 1998.

While in opposition, Labour had been critical of much of the Conservative Party's health policies. *Designed to Care* changed a great deal of the organisation of the health service. In it, Labour underlined its commitment to the main aims of the NHS in Scotland: that it be free at the point of use and open to all. Scottish Secretary Donald Dewar declared that *"this will be a NHS designed to co-operate, not compete, designed to deliver, not delay, and above all designed to care"*.

The main features of *Designed to Care* are:

◆ a commitment to cut waiting lists
◆ make £100 million in savings
◆ establish NHS Direct, a free phone enquiry service
◆ establish NHSnet to electronically link doctors' surgeries to create more co-operation

◆ introduce one-stop clinics to provide diagnoses, tests and results on the same day
◆ a commitment to raise public spending on health in real terms every year.

THE NHS IN THE NEW SCOTLAND

In May 1999, the Scottish Parliament assumed power over health. Unlike social security, health is a devolved power. This means that in the future, the NHS in Scotland is likely to become increasingly different from the NHS in England, Wales and Northern Ireland.

Health boards

Scotland has 15 regional health boards. Their role is to identify the health care needs of the people living in their area. They have the job of drawing up annual Health Improvement Programmes along with Acute NHS Trusts and Primary Care Trusts. The regional health board acts as a 'watchdog' in health standards and also takes an active role in promoting healthy living.

Acute Hospital Trusts

Each NHS hospital in Scotland is a Trust. Under the Conservatives, each Trust hospital acted like a business, competing for patients the way a business competes for customers. The Government believed that competition between the Trusts was good as it improved standards in health care. If a doctor could obtain a faster, better service for his patient in a different hospital, he could send the patient there. This, according to the theory of the 'internal market', would act as a signal to the rejected hospital to improve or update its service. It was believed that this would lead to a more efficient NHS with improved standards of care.

Labour abolished the internal market in April 1998. Today, Trust hospitals do not compete for patients, instead they co-operate together. Each hospital has the right to run its own affairs and make its own decisions, but it should do so after consulting other Acute NHS Trusts within the Health Board region. It is recommended that Acute Hospital Trusts should merge together in all areas, apart from Glasgow and Lothians. It is estimated that the number of hospitals in Scotland will drop to around 28, thereby making savings in management costs of around £110 million.

Primary Health Care Trusts

Primary care is the term used to describe health services that the patient comes into contact with directly. Doctors who are General Practitioners (GPs) and dentists are the main practitioners of primary care. Under the Conservatives, the controversial GP Fundholding scheme was set up. As with NHS Trusts, GPs could run their practice like a small business and compete for patients. GPs competed with each other to attract the most custom by offering the best quality of service. Labour abolished GP Fundholding in April 1998. In its place are the new Primary Care Trusts.

Primary Care Trusts are when GPs, community hospitals, mental health services and local authority social work departments join together. GPs, for example, will work closely with social workers to improve community care within a particular area. One success story of Primary Care Trusts has been the GP Out-of-Hours Service in Glasgow. Instead of all 622 GPs in Glasgow having to be on call at the same time, six centres have been set up across the city to deal with emergency out-of-hours situations. Out of the 622 GPs, 614 have taken part. The effect has been a reduction in costs and a quicker, more effective service for patients.

The Private Finance Initiative (PFI) and Public Private Partnership (PPS)

The Labour Government has not abandoned all of the Conservative's health care reforms. The PFI in health care is a scheme where the NHS will pay a private company (or companies joined together in a consortium) to build and maintain a new hospital. The advantage in the short term is that the Government (and the taxpayer) does not have to find funds to build a new hospital and the private company accepts all the risks and maintenance costs. The private company is responsible for the management of 'hotel' services within the hospital such as catering and cleaning. The Acute NHS Trust has responsibility for all clinical decisions. The disadvantage is that the Government always has to pay the private company rent for use of the hospital. It is claimed that this is a waste of money and it would be cheaper to borrow the money and pay it back over a number of years. Opinion on the merits of PFI is strongly debated between the political parties.

PFI is sometimes referred to as Public Private Partnership (PPS).

Today there are many PFI projects within the NHS, but there

THE NEW ROYAL INFIRMARY OF EDINBURGH

AND
ASSOCIATED UNIVERSITY OF EDINBURGH FACILITIES

The new Royal Infirmary of Edinburgh, built through the PFI

have been three large ones involving the building of new hospitals. Hairmyres Acute NHS Trust, near East Kilbride has been rebuilt under PFI at an estimated cost of £67.5 million; Law hospital, in Carluke has been built at a cost of £100 million and the new Edinburgh Royal Infirmary has been built at a cost of £180 million.

ACTIVITIES

1 Draw a spider diagram showing the main features of Designed to Care.
2 What is the role of Health Boards in the new NHS in Scotland?
3 What is meant by primary health care?
4 Sum up the main difference between GPs in GP fundholding practices and GPs in the new Primary Health Care Trusts? Give an example.
5 Explain the difference between an Acute Hospital Trust and a Primary Health Care Trust.
6 What are the advantages and disadvantages of the Private Finance Initiative?

THE ELDERLY IN THE UK

CASE STUDY

The elderly
"The best age is the age you are"
Maggie Kuhn, Founder of the Grey Panthers

The common stereotype of the elderly is of sad, moaning old people who love nothing better than being miserable. The comedian Harry Enfield has enjoyed caricaturing this stereotype in his sketch "The Old Gits". The fact that many elderly people find the sketch funny is evidence that the elderly, just like any other group of people, have a sense of humour. In fact, teenagers are just as likely as the elderly to suffer from '**ageism**'. This is the view that certain people of a certain age are all the same.

Unlike sexism and racism, ageism is not illegal. In 1998, the MP Linda Perham attempted to pass a Private Members Bill in the House of Commons that would make it illegal to place age restrictions on job advertisements. The Bill was defeated. The Government, however, has introduced a voluntary code of practice which businesses can agree to if they wish. Companies are encouraged not to use phrases such as 'young graduates' in job advertisements and to have mixed age interviewing panels. Some companies have moved faster than others. *B & Q, Marks and*

Spencer, Sainsbury's and the *Nationwide Building Society* have won particular praise from the Government in adopting fairer age employment practices. For a full copy of the code, contact: www.dfee.gov.uk/agediversity.

Definitions of 'youth' and 'elderly' have changed over time. Today, the official definition of elderly is 65 for men and 60 for women. This is the retirement age. In 2020, the retirement age will become 65 for both sexes. There is a distinction between being 'old' and being elderly. Being elderly is a fact. Being old is a matter of opinion. You may think your parents are 'old'. You may even think your teacher is 'old'. This is not necessarily so. They may lead a more active social life than you!

Obesity (fatness) has become a growing problem among young people. The growth of computer games, access to television, fear of traffic and of strangers in the street has led to a decline in activity for the young. By contrast, many 'old' people are taking up sport and leisure activities as they realise the social and health benefits of keeping fit. Improvements in education and medicine have enabled many who would have been 'old' in the past to remain active citizens.

ACTIVITIES

1 Give examples of ageist stereotypes that affect both young and older people.

2 Do you agree with the views of Maggie Kuhn? Give reasons for your answer.

3 Why might companies benefit from having a balance of different age groups in their employment?

4 Why has the gap between the lifestyles of young and older people narrowed in recent years?

In truth, age is all in the mind. Just as it would be ludicrous to believe that all people between the age of 12 and 19 are the same, those aged over 50 are very different, socially and economically.

THE ELDERLY TODAY

Demography is the study of changes in population. There has been a long-term increase in the numbers of elderly people in the UK.

Projections indicate that this trend will continue. In fact, by 2008, there will be more people over the retirement age than under the age of 16. This is the first time this has ever happened.

There are several reasons for this. These are detailed below.

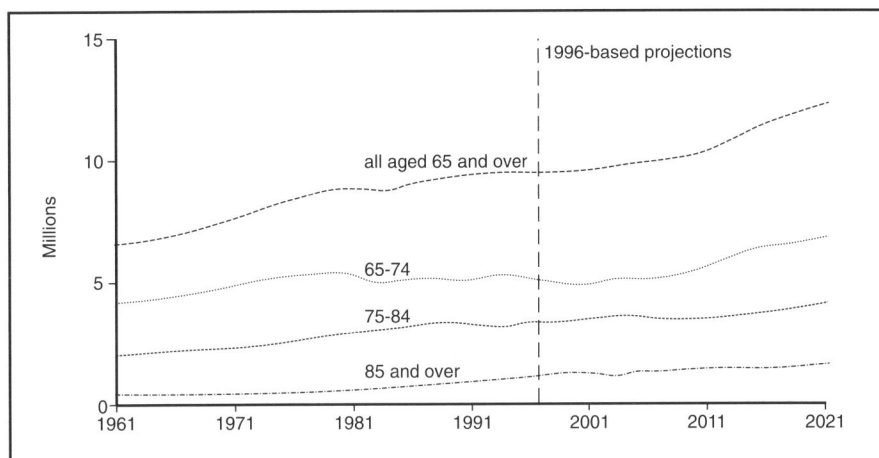

The numbers of elderly people are on the increase and are likely to continue increasing (Source: DSS, 1998)

Improved public health

Since the welfare state and the NHS were set up, there have been massive improvements in standards of public health for the vast majority of people. Diseases such as typhoid, TB, whooping cough and cholera are almost non-existent. These were major killers in the years before 1945.

No world wars

The wars of 1914–1918 and 1939–1945 took a heavy toll on the young generations of the time. Since then, while there have been wars involving British armed forces, there has been nothing like the carnage of the two world wars of the last century.

Breakthroughs in medical science

Vaccines and cures have been found for many killer diseases. As well as those previously mentioned, there have been important developments in the treatment of many types of cancer and other diseases affecting older people. One of the largest growth groups has been among the over 85s.

Family planning

Many families are deciding to have fewer children. Women are

Sophia Loren, aged 68

75

choosing to get married later and increasing numbers of women are having babies later. In addition, more women are choosing to have none at all. The availability of contraception and the declining influence of the church on the use of contraception have all combined to lower the birth rate.

ACTIVITIES

Draw a spider diagram which shows the reasons why there are more elderly people today.

IMPLICATIONS FOR YOUNG PEOPLE TODAY

The idea of the welfare state was to provide for all people from cradle to grave. Those in work, aged between 16 and 65, agreed to pay National Insurance contributions that would pay for benefits, including the retirement pension for those too young, too ill or too old to work. This unwritten agreement has been confronted by a demographical time bomb. While the numbers of elderly claiming State Retirement Pension (and other benefits) has gone up, the numbers of people available to work to pay for these benefits has gone down. As more elderly people are staying alive longer, inevitably many of those need to be cared for. This costs money. Politically, however, fewer people have been prepared to pay more in taxes to pay for state care for the elderly. The implications for the young of today are either pay more in tax or look after yourself by paying for your own pensions and health care.

WOOPIES AND POOR OLD SOULS

All pensioners saw their income rise between 1979 and 1996.

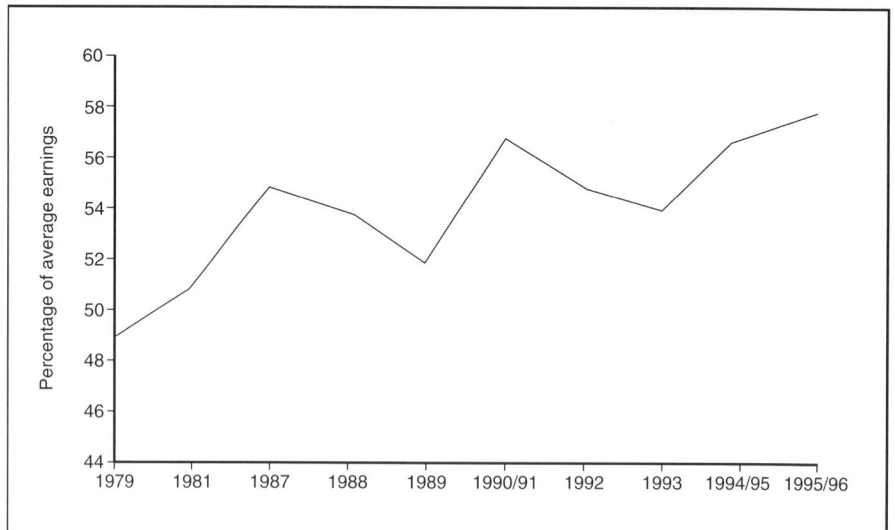

Pensioners' income compared to national average earnings (Source: DSS, 1998)

However, the average rise disguises the growing gulf between different groups of pensioners. The incomes of the poorest 10% of pensioners have grown by 31% in real terms since 1979. However, the richest 10%, the 'woopies', saw a larger real increase of 78% in their income. The 'Well Off Older Person' (woopy) is glad to be grey. On the other hand, the 'poor old souls' are not so well off.

1 What evidence is there that Frank Boag is a woopy?

2 What evidence is there that life is a struggle for Christine McPhee?

3 Compare the differences in lifestyle between Frank and Christine in

◆ income
◆ hobbies
◆ health
◆ housing

How did Frank Boag become a woopy?

Frank was lucky because he had a good job. His employer deducted a regular amount from his salary towards an Occupational Pension for him. This meant that when he retired in 1992, aged 60, Frank received 2/3 of his normal salary in the form of an occupational pension. His salary on retirement was £36,000. He also received a

Frank Boag is a woopy.		
Age	68	
Marital status	Married, to Betty	
Previous job	Architect	
Weekly income	Sept. 2000 figures	
	State retirement pension	£ 67.50
	Occupational pension	£300.00
	Private pension	£200.00
	Approx. total (does not include Betty's income or interest from savings, investments)	£567.50
Hobbies	Football (season ticket holder with Forfar Athletic and member of the Tartan Army). Enjoys holidays with his wife too.	
Health	Fit as a fiddle. Runs regularly. Plays golf.	
House	Detached bungalow. Mortgage paid off several years ago.	

Christine McPhee is a poor old soul.		
Age	68	
Marital status	Married to Bill	
Previous job	Housewife, did some part-time work	
Weekly income (combined with Bill)	2000 figures	
	Minimum Income Guarantee (MIG)	£121.95
	Attendance Allowance	£52.95
	Total	£174.90
Hobbies	Watching television. Likes reading.	
Health	Doesn't get out much. Suffers from bronchitis and agrophobia.	
Council house	Income Support pays rent. She likes her neighbours but struggles with the stairs.	

one-off 'lump sum' payment of £20,000. Frank also decided when he was younger that he wanted to retire early. He wanted to travel with Betty and spend time in the sun. He also wanted to go away with his Tartan Army friends! He therefore saved extra money in a private pension with a private pension firm. His 20 year long policy matured in 1993, providing him with an extra income.

Frank has always been lucky with his health. His job as an architect meant he got out and about. He did not have heavy weights to carry. He was not working with difficult people. While his job had its pressures, it was not as stressful as some others. His mortgage was paid off some years ago, meaning that he does not have to pay for his housing. He enjoys doing some gardening and DIY, but these are hobbies, not necessities. He can afford to pay for really big jobs around the house.

Frank's two daughters, Elisabeth and Susan, have just left university. Frank bought them a flat in Edinburgh to live in. He has now sold this, making a tidy profit.

Christine McPhee's story

Christine on the other hand has not been so fortunate. As Christine rarely worked, she did not have an occupational pension. Also, she was not entitled to the State Earnings Related Pension as she did not pay enough National Insurance contributions in her part-time job at the supermarket. She relies on Income Support to top up her state retirement pension. She has to be careful with her budget. She does not have expensive tastes as she is not fit enough to get out much. Her last holiday was a weekend with Bill in the Lake District last year.

Christine has been a 20-a-day smoker for over 40 years. She knows it is not good for her health, but claims she is 'too old' to stop now. She would like a new house, one without stairs, but there is a shortage of council sheltered housing available. Her health is not bad enough to make her a priority case. Christine's son, Mark, works in England. She does not see him as much as she would like to.

ACTIVITY

Extended writing

"*Young people today should start thinking about their pension.*"
Discuss this statement.

MEANS-TESTING: FOR AND AGAINST

The Government has recognised that many pensioners are in need. There are a variety of state benefits for elderly people. However, because the Government recognises that not all pensioners have the same needs, increasingly the benefits are means-tested, rather than universal. A **universal benefit** is something that all people receive. Child benefit, for example, is one of the few universal benefits. Today, most benefits are **means-tested**, which means that the individual only receives it if they are entitled to it. For example, Income Support is means-tested. It is available only to those pensioners who have less than £8000 in savings. It is argued that this penalises people who may have been careful with their money during their working life. Some believe that means-testing is degrading for people, especially the elderly, who have to claim benefits and prove that they are in need. Many elderly people do not like the personal questions involved in means-tested benefits. It is also claimed that as the elderly paid taxes while in work, they should receive the pay back now they are retired.

The Government, on the other hand, believes that means-testing is fairer because more benefits can be targeted at people who really need the help, such as Christine McPhee, rather than woopies such as Frank Boag. The Government has made the elderly more aware of the benefits that they are entitled to. The Government also make the economic case that as numbers of pensioners grow, especially well-off pensioners, the state simply cannot afford to pay everyone, regardless of need, the same benefits. Those who can afford to provide for themselves should provide for themselves and leave state benefits for those who really need them. The **Minimum Income Guarantee** was introduced specifically to help the poorest pensioners. The Labour Government claims that it has helped the poorest pensioners more than any other Government.

STATE BENEFITS FOR THE ELDERLY

- *Retirement Pension* – Entitlement is based on whether a person paid National Insurance contributions while at work.
- *Invalidity Allowance* – This is paid on top of the retirement pension, if a person received Invalidity Allowance before retiring.
- *Age Addition* – Those aged over 80 receive extra money.
- *Income Support* – For people on a low income. Those with savings over £3000 will have reduced Income Support and those with savings over £8000 are not eligible. Those on Income Support are entitled to Housing Benefit and Council Tax Benefit.
- *Attendance Allowance* – This is available to those over 65 who are too frail to look after themselves and have needed help for over six months.
- *Over 80 Pension* – Available to those aged over 80, who do not qualify for the retirement pension.
- *Free Television License* – Available to the over 75s.
- *Cold Weather Payments* – Paid during periods of very cold weather. There is no need to claim.
- *Winter Fuel Payments* – A one-off payment of £100 to help towards the heaviest fuel bill.
- *Christmas Bonus* – £10 per person.

Note: Benefits change very quickly. For the latest figures, contact the Benefits Agency at http://www.dss.gov.uk/ba.

ACTIVITIES

1 Explain the arguments for and against means-testing of benefits. "*The New Labour Government has done nothing for pensioners.*" Statement by Amanda Dargie.
2 Why could Amanda Dargie be accused of being selective in her use of facts?
3 Do you think the Government does enough for pensioners? Give reasons for your answer. If you think the Government should do more, explain where the money should come from.

GLAD TO BE GREY

"People over 50 today are fitter, more active and more adventurous than their parents' generation and while there remains enormous discrepancy in income between the richest and the poorest, overall this group controls 80% of the country's wealth and spends £145 billion a year".

Tim Bull, Strategic Planning Director, Saga

Saga Tours is a major global company. It sells many holidays to the over 50s age group, but it has used its successful brand name to expand to a whole range of other services to the 'woopy' market, such as house and health insurance. The company recognised, before many others, that the elderly were not all weak, frail and poor. Many elderly have a disposable income which they are keen to dispose of. A European advertising agency, *SeniorAgency*, discovered the following facts about the spending habits of the over 50s across the continent

The over 50s bought:

◆ 45% of all cars sold
◆ 80% of top-of-the-range cars
◆ 50% of face care cosmetics
◆ 80% of cruises

They were also interested in flowers, books, classical music, weekend flights, city visits and concerts.

However, 97% of all advertising spending was dedicated to the under-50 customers. It concluded that many companies were ageist in their attitudes towards elderly people. Companies were frightened of being labelled 'old'. Advertising managers as a group were also younger people and held stereotyped ideas about age. Elderly people, despite their wealth, had become the 'forgotten consumers'.

ACTIVITY

Design a product that would have appeal for an over-50 audience. State the name of the product, its price and why you believe it would be popular with this market audience. Draw a poster that could be used in a glossy magazine to promote your product.

HOUSING FOR THE ELDERLY

Contrary to stereotype, the majority of elderly people live independently at home.

In England and Wales, the number of elderly people who are owner–occupiers is far higher than in Scotland.

Sheltered housing

Out of a total UK pensioner population of 10.5 million, 7 million are women. Loneliness and isolation can therefore be a problem. The elderly, like everyone else, wish to be independent and be in control of their life. However, living alone, particularly for poor pensioners who may live in an unsuitable local home, can be a concern. One solution is **sheltered housing**. This can be a good solution for some elderly people. Sheltered housing is not the same as a nursing home. In a sheltered house, the resident has their own front door and complete privacy. There is a warden available 24 hours a day in case of emergency. The house is often part of a complex of houses, most of which are on one level. The homes are fitted with the elderly in mind, with easier access to baths and plug points that are easy to reach. As usual, resources are the problem. Local authorities would like to build more sheltered housing, but do not have the money. Only 4% of people aged over 60 in Scotland live in sheltered housing.

According to *Help the Aged* (www.helptheaged.org.uk), the priority for the Government should be to ensure that the elderly in all types of housing are safe and warm. 96% of properties with no central heating are occupied by older householders. If you are a poor pensioner with health problems, a large part of your life will be spent indoors. Heating costs in the winter are likely to take up a large part of your weekly budget. It takes 66% more fuel to heat a house in Braemar than it does in Bristol.

Older people are much more likely to live in housing that is below the tolerable standard. According to Strathclyde Elderly Forum, 90% of pensioners in Scotland live in a house requiring some kind of repair.

Relative fuel costs in the UK

ACTIVITIES

1 What evidence is there that Scottish pensioners have greater needs than others in the UK?
2 Why might sheltered housing be a good solution for a single elderly person?
3 Why do so few elderly people live in sheltered housing?

Residential care and nursing homes

> **BlairAdam Residential Home**
> ◆ Comfortable and spacious private rooms.
> ◆ All rooms en-suite with direct dial phone and remote control digital television.
> ◆ Loyal, dedicated staff. All our nurses and assistants are qualified professionals.
> ◆ Entertainments programme to suit all.
> ◆ Unrestricted visiting. Residents may bring any personal belongings and furniture.

A residential care home can be provided by the local authority Social Work Department, or a private or voluntary organisation. It is a type of home where residents live and meals and care is provided. All homes have to be registered with the local authority and can be regularly inspected.

A nursing home has all of the above facilities, but in addition has the constant care and supervision of qualified nursing staff. A nursing home has to be staffed 24 hours a day by trained nurses. Some residential homes will allow day care, either to improve the quality of life for the elderly person on a temporary basis, or offer some respite for a regular carer.

If the elderly person has assets of over £16,000 (1999 figures) they can make their own arrangements independently. If assets are lower than £16,000, or become lower than £16,000, an assessment will be carried out by the Social Work Department to decide whether the person meets the criteria for state help to enter a residential home.

Medical and financial criteria
- The elderly person is seen to be at unreasonable risk in their own home.
- The elderly person has needs that can only be met in residential care.
- The main carer of the elderly person cannot continue helping without risking their own health.

The Social Work Department will also take into account the individual's financial situation. If the individual has less than £10,000 in savings, they may be asked to pay a nominal amount. Income Support may be available. If savings are between £10,000 and £16,000, the amount charged may vary. In 1998, full charges for a residential care home run by Fife Council were £382 per week. Many in the private sector are more expensive. Fife Social Work Department paid a maximum of £249 per week for a person to take a single room in a private residential care home.

Care in the community

Many elderly people, to varying degrees, are cared for in the community. A Community Care assessment is carried out by the Social Work Department. A person would be eligible for community care if they had:
- a disabling illness
- a terminal illness
- a sensory impairment
- HIV or AIDS
- drug or alcohol problems
- a physical disability
- mental health problems, including dementia
- learning disabilities.

One of the main principles of Care in the Community is to avoid putting the individual into institutional care, either in hospital or a

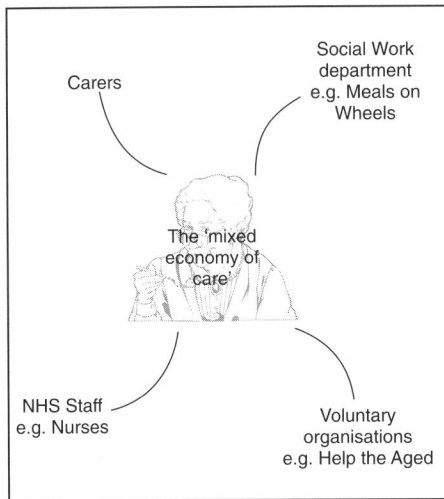

The "mixed economy of care"

residential home. Under community care, the care comes to the individual, rather than the other way around. It has many advantages. The main advantage of community care is that the individual can stay in the comfort of their home, near to neighbours and familiar surroundings. That is a choice the individual makes. Most people would rather live at home and lead as normal a life as possible. Various people and organisations will provide the care.

Carers are nominated people who take a special interest in the well being of the elderly person. It can be a member of the family or a friend or neighbour. Carers must have access to a certain amount of time off, and alternative care or respite care provided as a replacement.

While few people dispute the advantages of good community care, there have been criticisms of the system in practise. There have been complaints that it has been used as a cost-saving device by the Government. Carers have complained of not having enough respite. Indeed, who cares for the carers? Many carers have become ill through the pressure of looking after a needy elderly person. With all the different organisations involved, community care takes a great deal of planning to be a success, and it is very easy for something to go wrong and the elderly person to miss out on care.

ACTIVITIES

1 What is meant by the 'mixed economy of care'?
2 What are the advantages of Care in the Community?
3 What criticisms have been made of Care in the Community?

THE GREY PANTHERS

The Black Panthers were an organisation which fought for the rights of African–Americans in the 1960s. Today there are hundreds of organisations called the *Grey Panthers* across North America. They have been formed to campaign for improved living standards for elderly people. The growth of Grey Panther organisations reflects the growing awareness among elderly people of their strength in numbers. If well organised, the elderly can be a powerful economic and political pressure group. In Scotland, the main Grey Panthers are the networks of Elderly Forums, the largest of which is Strathclyde Elderly Forum.

Strathclyde Elderly Forum has three main aims:
◆ To *inform* older people about the issues that affect them.
◆ To *empower* older people to stand up for themselves.
◆ To *campaign* for better rights, services and facilities for older people.

Informing
Strathclyde Elderly Forum launched its website in May 1998. It can be found at www.StrathclydeElderlyForum.org.uk. It seeks to inform elderly people of their rights and the services that are available. Through regular public meetings in local communities, the Forum puts elderly people in touch with advisers about issues such as housing and social security benefits.

Empowering
The Forum aims to challenge the view that elderly people are

powerless victims. It seeks to make elderly people aware that there are others in similar circumstances and that change is possible through working together. All the leading members of the Forum are over 60. While the Forum has made links and good relations with people of all ages, including students, it is essentially an organisation *of* elderly people, *for* elderly people.

Campaigning

There are many examples of the campaigning activities of the Forum. The Forum has issued a Pensioners' Charter which demands improvements in health services, housing and transport facilities.

In 1998, it wrote to every MP asking them to support an increase in the State Retirement Pension that reflected a rise in general salaries, rather than a rise in prices. Since 1979, the pension has risen in proportion to the rise in prices, which has been lower than the national rise in earnings. It also wrote to MPs asking for their support in voting for the Private Members Bill of Linda Perham MP which tried to make ageism illegal. The Forum, together with other Scottish Grey Panther groups, lobbied the Scottish Office in 1998.

ACTIVITIES

1 Draw a spider diagram showing the aims of Strathclyde Elderly Forum.
2 Why do politicians have to listen to the voice of elderly people?
3 Give examples of the methods used by Strathclyde Elderly Forum to achieve its aims.

3

CRIME AND THE LAW IN SOCIETY

This chapter has a strong emphasis on the **Scottish legal and criminal justice system**, and will:

◆ examine the changing trends in criminal behaviour
◆ describe the priorities of the Scottish Executive in tackling crime
◆ examine policing methods in Scotland
◆ discuss the fairness of the Scottish court system
◆ debate the different methods of punishing young offenders
◆ examine how society has responded to the challenges of car and drug crime.

Jonathan Aitken, disgraced former cabinet minister

"We shall be tough on crime and tough on the causes of crime."

Tony Blair

LAW

We all have to obey rules. We may not always like these rules, but we have to obey them. If we choose not to, we have to accept the consequences of our actions. In school there are rules, such as not speaking while the teacher is talking. Choosing to break this rule will usually involve some kind of punishment. Teachers have to obey rules as well. For example, it is against the law for a teacher to hit pupils. A teacher who did, and was found guilty of doing so, would be punished. Even the most powerful people in the land have to obey rules. In 1998, the former Conservative Cabinet Minister Jonathan Aitken was found guilty of perjury (telling lies in court). He was sent to jail.

The vast majority of us choose to obey rules and laws, because the alternative would be chaos (or anarchy). Imagine if there were no rules on road safety. Anyone at any age could drive. People could drive on any side of the road; with or without lights; sober or drunk; at any speed. Without laws to protect us we would be at the mercy of people who could harm us or steal our property.

The UK does not have one legal system. England and Wales, Scotland and Northern Ireland each have their own legal systems. This means that while there are some laws which apply throughout the UK, others will be different in each of the countries within the UK. England and Wales, Scotland and Northern Ireland each have their different court systems and police structures. In Scotland, for example, it is legal to be married at 16 without parental consent. In England, the minimum age for marriage without parental consent is 18.

There are two types of law throughout the UK: criminal law and civil law.

CRIMINAL LAW

This is a crime which affects the community and a person charged with breaking the criminal law will be charged under criminal law. Criminal laws are very serious. Murder and violent assault are criminal charges and punishments can often be severe.

CIVIL LAW

This is to set rules between people. For example, in the buying and selling of a house, there are rules which must be obeyed. The purpose of civil law is to settle any dispute between people, where one (or more) may have broken the law. Unlike criminal law, the aim of civil law is not to punish those who have broken the law, but to provide compensation for the person(s) who have been unjustly treated.

There are often 'grey areas' between the two types of crime and overlaps can happen. Crimes such as 'anti-social' behaviour from a neighbour is a civil crime against a person, but the anti-social neighbour may also be committing criminal acts e.g. drug taking and/or dealing. Other examples could include the crime of harassment which is a civil crime, but would also involve criminal behaviour. In this case, the neighbour may be charged under the Crime and Disorder Act and appear before a Criminal Court. However, the offended neighbour may also wish to sue the anti-social neighbour for loss or damage. In this case, the charge would appear before a civil court.

DEMOCRATIC CITIZENSHIP

In the UK, most people choose to obey the law because we have a say in the making, the interpretation, even the enforcement of the law. This is what is meant by 'democratic citizenship'.

Democratic citizenship means being aware of your rights to make decisions, interpret decisions and enforce decisions. It also means being aware of your responsibilites towards other people and society as a whole.

We have a say in the making of laws because we elect those who make the laws which affect us. We elect Members of the European Parliament (MEPs) who help to make European law. We elect Members of the House of Commons (MPs) who make laws affecting the UK. We elect members of the Scottish Parliament (MSPs) who make legislation affecting Scotland. We also elect local councillors who can make local laws, called 'by-laws'. We can take part simply by voting. If we feel strongly enough about issues, we can help political parties by joining and helping with their activities.

In between elections, we have the right to influence law makers. We can write to newspapers. We can form pressure groups to lobby MSPs. We can telephone radio and television shows with our points of view. We can now e-mail MSPs on issues that concern us and expect a reply. Ultimately, we have the right to stand for parliament ourselves if we feel strongly enough.

Whilst we have these democratic rights, we also have responsibilities. We have to accept the majority result in an election, even if our choice did not win. We have to obey laws that we do not agree with. If we join a pressure group, we have the responsibility to obey the law during democratic protest. If we choose not to, we have to accept the penalties of fines, community service, even prison.

Cash for questions – an abuse of democracy

In 1995, two Conservative MPs, Neil Hamilton and Tim Smith, were accused of taking money to ask questions in the House of Commons on behalf of their 'clients'. This was seen as an abuse of the trust that constituents place in their representatives. The affair became known as the 'Cash for Questions' scandal. Tim Smith resigned from office, but Neil Hamilton stayed on, protesting his innocence. BBC reporter Martin Bell felt so strongly about the issue that he stood against Neil Hamilton in his constituency of Tatton in the 1997 General Election. He stood as an 'independent anti-sleaze candidate'. He had, and still has, no political party. He won and has remained the MP for for Tatton, representing the constituents on his own, without any political party.

Neil Hamilton (left) and Martin Bell (right)

It is up to the courts to interpret the law, and we have a say in this too. In criminal law juries are drawn from members of the public. No person will go to jail without a trial by their peers. In interpreting the law we have the responsibility of being objective. It is the job of a public jury to honestly consider the facts, without bias or prejudice.

The police enforce the law and it is our right to have protection under the law. We elect local councillors who advise the police on aspects of police policy. We have the right to remain silent if arrested and the right to legal representation and a fair trial by a jury of our peers. We also have the responsibility to be honest and to co-operate with the police in law enforcement. We have the responsibility to inform the police if we are aware of crimes being committed and not to lie during police investigations.

1 Give examples of rules in your school.
2 Which do you obey
a) because you agree with them?
b) because the consequences of disobeying them would be worse?
3 If you have a pupil council, explain how it has helped make the school more democratic.
4 Explain the difference between criminal and civil laws.
5 Explain what is meant by 'democratic citizenship'. Give examples.
6 Are you a democratic citizen? Why/Why not?

THE LAW MAKERS

A number of institutions make laws which affect us. These range from local councillors who meet in our local town halls to members of the European Parliament who meet in Strasbourg and Brussels.

THE EUROPEAN UNION

All UK laws can be challenged under European Community law. Under the Treaty of Rome, which the UK signed in 1973 when it joined the EU, the European Court of Justice is the supreme law-making body. If a disagreement occurs between UK law and European law, it is European community law that will be the most powerful. One of the best examples is the banning of corporal punishment in schools. Practises such as the belting of badly-behaved pupils were legal in the UK until 1981, when a Scottish parent raised her objections at the European Court of Human Rights. The Court agreed with the objection and all corporal punishment has been banned in the UK since 1981.

In 1998, the House of Commons passed the Human Rights Act. This means that the rights contained in the European Convention of Human Rights (ECHR) have to be part of UK law. In England, the Convention did not come into force until October 2000, but it came into force in Scotland on 20 May 1999. Laws made by the Scottish Parliament also have to abide by the European Convention.

In November 1999, the first conflict arose between the Convention and practises and the Scottish legal system. Article 6 of the Convention states that *"everyone is entitled to a fair and public hearing by an independent and impartial tribunal"*. In Scotland, not all sheriffs had full-time, permanent jobs. Due to the number of court cases, the Lord Advocate, Lord Hardie, who was a member of the Scottish Executive and also represents the prosecution, had appointed temporary judges in sheriff courts. The Linlithgow lawyer, Jim Keegan, representing two youths charged with assault claimed that the temporary sheriff David Crowe should not try the case. As a temporary sheriff, he was appointed by the prosecution and Jim Keegan felt his clients would not be given an impartial trial under European Law. It was alleged that temporary sheriffs might be biased to support the prosecution in order to get a permanent job. Many lawyers see a spell as a temp as a way of securing a permanent job as a well paid permanent sheriff (£92,000 per year and pension). Appointment to sheriff is made by the Lord Advocate.

The historic appeal by the three Linlithgow lawyers was upheld in the Court of Appeal. Lord Cullen announced that the use of temporary sheriffs appointed by the Lord Advocate breached Article 6 of the European Convention. This caused a crisis in the Scottish legal system. The Scottish Executive, and Justice Minister Jim Wallace in particular, was embarrassed. In theory, all those convicted under temporary sheriffs between May and November 1999 could appeal against their convictions. Some claimed that "the gates of Barlinnie will burst open".

In hindsight, it was a bad error for the Scottish Executive to make, but until the three lawyers raised the appeal, no-one had foreseen how the European Convention would affect this Scottish practice. Further challenges to Scottish law, including possibly the Children's Hearing system, are expected in years to come. In many ways, the end result may be that Scotland will have a written constitution, based on the European Convention.

The Convention has a number of articles which describe the rights that young people have. For example, Article 20 gives children the right to care by the Government if their family cannot looking after them. The Convention emphasises the rights of the child but also the need to respect other people.

ACTIVITIES

1   Match up the following rights with their responsibilities:

Rights:	Responsibilities:
To be protected from drugs and drug dealing.	Not to be offensive to the feelings of other people.
To go to school.	To consider other points of view and beliefs.
To decide your own beliefs and feelings.	To support the police in the fight against drugs.
To express yourself in different ways e.g. art, writing.	To consider the privacy of others.
To play, leisure and recreation.	To work to the best of your ability and consider others.

2 Give three examples of rights that you have under the European Convention of Universal Human Rights. What responsibilities do you think go along with these rights?

3 Give examples of conflicts between UK law and European law.

4 Why did the Keegan case cause a crisis in the Scottish legal system?

DEFINITIONS OF CRIME

The definition of crime changes over time. What used to be a crime in the past is not necessarily a crime now. For example, treason is still a crime in Britain. In theory, it is still punishable by death. In the past, a person who criticised a member of the Royal Family could have been found guilty of treason and executed. This does not happen now!

The reason the definition of crime changes is because there is a strong connection between what people feel is 'right' and 'wrong'. The law reflects what society believes to be right. It punishes those that society feels to have committed wrong. What is 'right' and 'wrong' in the eyes of society changes through time.

The punishment for murder in the UK used to be murder. In many countries it still is. Everyone has a sense of 'justice'. Capital punishment in its various forms is increasingly used in the USA. Today in the UK, a convicted murderer will receive a life-time imprisonment. This is because society's views on crime and punishment have changed. Scottish school teachers used to use 'corporal punishment' against pupils who broke school rules. Pupils are no longer physically punished for wrong-doing. Again, this is because of a change in society's attitude towards crime and punishment.

ACTIVITY

Organise a class debate on the motion:

"This class believes that Scotland would be a better place if we restored corporal and capital punishment".

Even if you do not take part in the debate, you can still do a piece of extended writing. Follow the hamburger method for both the debate and the extended writing task.

These beliefs are called moral values. We all have moral values about things we believe are 'right' and things we believe are 'wrong'. It is the job of lawmakers to try to reflect the moral values of the people during election time and to make laws which will please the majority of the people. Some people are 'floating voters'. This means that what they feel is right varies from election to election. Their vote may not be based on deeply held morals, but pragmatism – what is in their best personal interests at any given moment. Others, however, are committed to a particular set of ideas (ideology) which a political party represents. They are likely to have a strong sense of loyalty to that party.

MORAL VALUES AND THE LAW

There is, however, a strong difference between a moral value and a law. It is possible to break a moral value, but not break a law. For example, a man having an affair behind his girlfriend's back may well be 'doing the dirty', but assuming his other girlfriend is a grown, responsible adult, this would not be illegal. Likewise, it is possible to break the law, yet not feel guilty. The law merely attempts to reflect society's major moral values. In the UK, this traditionally has reflected Christian teachings (e.g. the Ten Commandments). Britain, however, is a democracy and understands that not all people agree on all moral issues. The UK is increasingly a multicultural country, where there are many different faiths and some who have no organised set of religious beliefs. If a society imposed one set of moral/religious teachings, it would not be a democracy, but a 'theocracy'.

ACTIVITIES

1 Give an example of an action which you believe to be immoral but not illegal. Give another which you believe to be illegal but not immoral.
2 Give an example of a law, or government policy, you feel has a basis in religious belief.

CRIME IN THE UK

Crime statistics are recorded by the Government and analysed by the police. In Scotland in 1996, the number of recorded crimes fell for the fifth successive year. In 1998, 432 000 crimes were committed in Scotland. This was an increase from 1997, the first increase since 1992. There was also a total of 516 000 'offences'. An offence is dealt with separately because most offenders are caught in the act, e.g. speeding motorists. The prosecution (or 'clear-up') rate is therefore far higher.

Officially, crime comes under several categories:

1 **Non-sexual Crimes of Violence**
This would include murder, serious assault, the handling of offensive weapons and robbery. This category of crime was on the increase in 1998, especially handling an offensive weapon, which was up by 13%.
2 **Crimes of Indecency (including sexual crimes)**
This type of crime would include assault, prostitution and 'lewd and indecent behaviour'. There was an increase in recorded crime in this category by 4% during the year. The figure of 7400 is the highest since 1971.
3 **Crimes of Dishonesty**
These include housebreaking, car theft, shoplifting and fraud. The number of crimes of theft involving 'opening a lockfast place' show a dramatic increase of 26%. Car thefts are on the decrease and numbered 28 400 in 1998.
4 **Crimes of Vandalism**
These crimes fell in 1998. Crimes of malicious mischief fell by 2% (1600) and crimes of fire-raising fell by 10% (2500) in 1998.
5 **"Other Crimes"**
This chiefly involves drug-related crime. This increased by 7% in 1998 to 29,400 cases. This is four times the number in 1989.

ACTIVITIES

"*Crime in Scotland is getting worse all the time.*" Statement by *Dougie Black.*
1 What evidence is there that Dougie Black is being selective in his use of facts?
2 Draw graphs showing the reported crimes that are going up and those going down.

Sociologists also classify a crime according to its meaning in society. These are unofficial classifications which may lead us to a better understanding of why certain people are more likely to commit certain crimes than others.

'White collar crime'

This is non-violent crime that is committed by 'respectable' people with responsible jobs. It includes business fraud such as tax evasion or computer hacking. Many people do not see tax evasion as a crime. Indeed there is a thin legal line between tax *avoidance* and tax *evasion*. It is the job of accountants to advise companies of the legal difference. Individuals may be involved in white collar crime by fiddling expenses or making fraudulent insurance claims.

'Blue collar crime'

These are crimes which tend to be committed by those at the lower end of our class system. They will usually involve crimes of robbery, violence and drugs. Sociologists have commented that these types of crimes have been punished more severely by courts than white collar crimes. This may be because the crimes are more 'visible' – they tend to attract tabloid media attention. It may also be due to a bias in the legal system. The offenders may not have as high a status as white collar criminals in the eyes of the legal profession. It may be that these crimes affect ordinary people more directly than professional crime and tougher examples are set by the courts.

Organised crime

Courts tend to draw a distinction between those who commit crimes in an organised, calculating manner and those who commit them by accident or temptation ('opportunistic crime'). A gang of drug dealers, shoplifters or armed robbers will be dealt with severely by the courts. The organised murder of a person will receive the highest punishment. The unorganised or accidental killing of a person is described as manslaughter. This is a serious crime, but will not be punished with the same severity as organised crime. Likewise a person who stole because of a moment of weakness will not be punished as severely as a calculated 'professional' thief.

Political crime

Republican or Loyalist terrorists have been involved in violent attacks, murders, even drug-related and sexual crimes. They have justified their actions by claiming there is a 'political' motive for their crimes. In 1981, 10 IRA men died on hunger strike because the Government was treating them as 'ordinary' criminals rather than 'political prisoners'. In 1998, the Omagh bombing, carried out by the 'Real IRA', killed dozens of innocent people and injured many more. The Loyalist gang, the 'Shankhill Butchers', has also killed many who had no connection with terrorist groups. The Good Friday Peace agreement in Northern Ireland has aroused controversy as 'political' prisoners have been released from jail while 'ordinary' prisoners have remained inside to complete their sentence.

ACTIVITIES

1 Give examples of the following types of crime:
◆ white collar
◆ blue collar
◆ organised
◆ political.
2 Why may some types of crime be punished more severely than others?

Viewpoint A

"The release of paramilitary prisoners is part and parcel of achieving peace in Northern Ireland. They have not been pardoned. They have been released on a promise of good behaviour and will be re-imprisoned if they offend. They are not normal prisoners. In a normal society these people would not be members of paramilitary organisations. Peace is more important than punishment".

Viewpoint B

"It disgusts me to see convicted killers walk free. Burglars are still in jail, while organised, sometimes serial, killers are now walking the streets just because they claim a 'political cause' for their crimes. They made a choice to join banned, illegal organisations and to break the law. They should serve their time in jail".

3 Describe the differences between Viewpoint A and Viewpoint B on political crime.
4 Which point of view do you agree with most? Give reasons for your answer.

Is crime on the increase?

There is a common perception that we live in a more dangerous, violent country than we used to. Elderly people may reflect on a more law-abiding, honest age than we have at the moment. Crime *may* be on the increase. Officially, certain crimes *are* on the increase, but we must be careful in interpreting the evidence. There is a famous phrase *"there are lies, damned lies and statistics"*. This means that statistics can be misleading or selective in their use of facts. They may not tell the whole story. This is especially the case with crime statistics. This is because it is important to draw a difference between actual crime and recorded crime. Criminal statistics tell us the *recorded* crimes that have been reported to the police. This may lead us to think that crime is going up when all that is happening is that it may be recorded more.

Why crime may be recorded more

◆ The police are becoming increasingly sophisticated in their job. The use of new technology, such as computers and CCTV cameras, are allowing the police to find out about more criminal acts. In the past, we may not have known about them taking place.
◆ More property crimes are being reported now because more

people have insurance. For example, for a burglar victim to receive compensation from an insurance company, the police must be informed. As more people today have more valuable possessions in the house, and these are increasingly insured, more crimes may be being reported than before.

♦ Society's values change. Certain crimes in the past such as sexual crimes were 'taboo' subjects. Women who may have been sexually assaulted used to feel that the crime was 'their fault'. Similarly, children who may have been abused may have felt the same. Because of public education and the police becoming more professional in helping the victims of these crimes, perhaps there is not more crime being committed, perhaps more crime is being reported.

♦ There is greater confidence in the justice system. More racial crimes are being reported now. Perhaps this is because victims feel more confident that their views will be listened to by the courts and that the offender(s) will be punished. It does not necessarily mean that more 'hate crimes' are being committed.

ACTIVITIES

1 What is the difference between recorded crime figures and 'real crime' figures?
2 Why may crime be recorded more now than in the past? Give examples.

THE CAUSES OF CRIME

Social scientists have long debated the causes of crime. There are strengths and weaknesses in the different explanations.

Poverty

Certain crimes, such as car theft, drug abuse and violent assault, are highest in poorer areas of town. Similarly, more criminals and prisoners come from working class backgrounds than middle class backgrounds. Some sociologists would say that some crime can be explained by coming from a 'socially excluded' background. Because young children may have parents who are poor role models, they may grow up not respecting the law. Similarly if the school environment is tough, children may learn that violence is the way to achieve things. There may be strong peer group pressure to be 'hard' or challenge authority. Likewise, if a person has low educational ability and/or a lack of qualifications, the temptation to commit crime may be very strong. The growing divide in Britain between the 'haves' and the 'have-nots' may mean a rise in crimes because some people may have nothing to lose by breaking the law. Deprived housing estates may be 'breeding grounds' for crime.

There is certainly a strong connection between low income, poor housing, lack of education and crime. Some sociologists, however, would state that this does not explain why some people from the same poor backgrounds are perfectly law abiding. To answer this, we have to look at more personal psychological reasons for why people commit crimes.

Affluence

This may explain white collar crime. Professional, educated people may commit crimes because they are well off and want to become more well off! Today's society places a lot of importance on material possessions such as having the right car, the right clothes and the right house. Individuals may feel under pressure to 'keep up with the Jones's' and commit crimes of fraud to finance an affluent lifestyle.

Individualist theories

These claim that certain people do not have the same ideas of 'right' and 'wrong' as other people. Crime cannot be blamed on 'society', but on individuals who are either too weak to obey the law or have made deliberate choices to be criminal. Because of events that may have taken place in childhood, they may commit serious crimes and not feel guilt about committing them. In extreme cases, such as sexual offenders, such people may not be able to be 'cured' by the traditional methods of fines or imprisonment but need psychiatric attention, perhaps all their life.

Traditionally in the UK, the Conservative Party used to be seen as the 'law and order party'. It believed in the individualist theory. 'Tougher' punishments were necessary for offenders to teach them a lesson and also to frighten off potential offenders. Crimes were committed because society was not tough enough on offenders, who believed they could 'get away with it'. The Conservatives traditionally believed in policies such as increasing police powers, capital/corporal punishment and tough prison rules, and were dismissive of 'excuses' made by criminals.

By contrast, 'Old Labour' tended to look to faults in society to explain criminal behaviour. Labour traditionally blamed lack of opportunities in society for crimes such as vandalism and burglary. For white collar crime, it pointed to the 'greed' encouraged by capitalist society. The punishments Old Labour favoured were those which emphasised changing the individual's circumstances rather than punishment.

Tony Blair changed this emphasis in his phrase *"tough on crime, tough on the causes of crime"*. New Labour now believes in traditionally Conservative policies such as 'strong' police tactics and 'tough' punishments but it also looks to the Old Labour solution of tackling the 'causes' of crime, such as poverty.

THE SCOTTISH EXECUTIVE

It is the job of the Scottish Executive to set the priorities for crime and the legal system. It will take time for the new Scottish Executive to develop new solutions for crime which are appropriate for Scotland. The 1999 Labour/Liberal Democrat coalition has closely followed the priorities of the UK Labour Government. It has adopted Tony Blair's approach which New Labour promised in its 1997 General Election manifesto:

ACTIVITIES

1 Draw a spider diagram showing the possible causes of crime.
2 What differences are there between the different theories of crime?
3 Which theory, if any, do you agree with most? Give reasons for your answer.
4 Why do you think New Labour changed from Labour's old attitude towards crime?

Extended writing

Present a four page report on 'Crime and the Law':
Page 1 – Explain the different types of crime.
Page 2 – Are people born 'bad'?
Page 3 – Why do criminals commit crimes?
Page 4 – How does crime affect people?
Use the BBC Scotland audio tape *Crime and the Law*, programme 1.

Establish a ban on the private ownership of handguns

In the aftermath of the Dunblane tragedy in 1996, when the new Labour Government came into power in 1997 it quickly passed a law banning the private ownership of handguns. An amnesty was allowed, whereby people had time to hand in any guns to the police. After this time, it would be an offence to own such a gun. A total of 6259 weapons were handed over to the police. Britain now has some of the toughest gun laws in the world.

Create a new Drug Enforcement Agency (DEA)

The UK wide DEA was set up in 1999. Keith Hellawell was appointed as national co-ordinator or the 'drugs Czar' as he has become known. The DEA seeks to bring together the best national practices in combating drugs. This will range from the sharing of information between UK police forces in capturing drugs and drug dealers to the best educational methods in promoting the anti-drugs message.

Introduce the Crime and Disorder Act

This is a wide-ranging law which aims to clamp down on 'low level' crimes which can cause a great deal of distress to the public. The focus is on punishing a variety of anti-social forms of behaviour. In 1999, over 50% of calls made to Strathclyde Police concerned 'nuisance' crimes such as the playing of loud music, drunkenness, vandalism, littering and under-age drinking. The Crime and Disorder Act has brought in a new offence of racial harassment. It also gives councils and the police powers to control 'neighbours from hell'. The police can now seize hi-fi equipment if it is a nuisance and councils can evict violent or noisy neighbours much earlier under the new Anti-Social Behaviour Orders.

Establish a network of Crime Prevention and Community Safety projects

By 2000, £5 million had been spent on establishing closed circuit television (CCTV) schemes. CCTV has been very effective in deterring criminal behaviour in areas where violent crime had been common. The *Crimestoppers* campaign allows members of the public to use free, confidential phone lines.

Reduce domestic violence

This follows the high profile zero tolerance campaigns used by many local authorities to highlight the problem of domestic violence. Education in schools and community groups has been carried out. The Government has been encouraged by the way that drink driving is no longer seen as acceptable behaviour. It is hoping that it can change public attitudes in a similar way over domestic violence. To do this, the Scottish Executive has set up a 'taskforce' called the Scottish Partnership on Domestic Violence. It aims to work at long-term education to change attitudes, and in the short term, to provide more help for women, especially in rural communities or from poor backgrounds, who may be the victims of domestic violence.

Seek alternatives to custodial sentences

There are many people in jail in Scotland who are not violent. While they have been found guilty of criminal acts, they do not pose a violent threat to the public. Jail is a costly use of the nation's resources. It has also been found to be counter-productive, as many prisoners do not change their criminal behaviour after leaving jail. There have also been a number of suicides involving women at Cornton Vale prison in Stirling. It is a Government priority to punish criminals in the community wherever possible, so long as they pose no physical threat to the public. Strategies such as electronic tagging of offenders have been introduced.

Attack social exclusion

The Scottish Executive believes that poverty is the main, although not the only, cause of crime. The definition of poverty has been widened to include not just financial poverty, but a lack of education, social skills, health, power and hope. This is termed 'social exclusion'. The Executive believes that if it can reduce unemployment, reduce school exclusion and improve life-long education, it can reduce the level of crime. This is known as the Social Exclusion strategy. It is explained in greater detail in Chapter Two. It means that the Government can claim to be tackling not just the effects of crime, but the underlying causes of crime.

EXTENSION

Listen to the BBC Scotland audio tape *Crime and the Law*, programme 2 and write a four page report on 'Enforcing the law'.

Page 1 – Explain the different punishments available in Scotland.

Page 2 – Describe life in a Young Offender's Institution (page 114).

Page 3 – Debate whether criminals should be helped or punished.

Page 4 – How can crime be prevented?

ACTIVITIES

1   Describe the priorities of the Scottish Executive in tackling crime.
2   Draw a spider diagram which explains 'social exclusion'.

Extended writing

"*New Labour's solutions to crime are just the same as the Conservative's.*"
Discuss this statement.

THE POLICE

It is the job of the police to enforce the law and protect the public. Ideally this means preventing crime before it happens. However, if a crime does happen, it is the duty of the police to investigate the crime and bring the accused to justice before a court of law, if required.

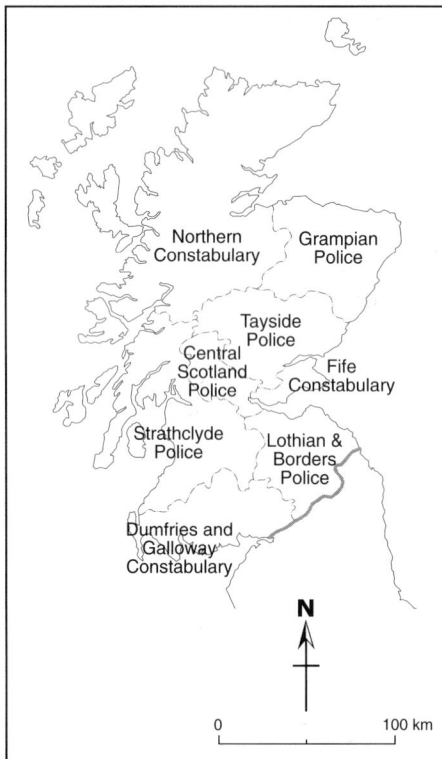

A map of the eight Scottish police forces

Jim Wallace, MSP Scotland's first Minister for Home Affairs

STRUCTURE OF THE POLICE

Decisions affecting the police are made by the Home Office in England and Wales and by the Scottish Executive in Scotland. The Northern Ireland Office sets priorities for its own police force. In England and Wales, the Home Secretary sets 'key policing objectives' for the 43 police forces.

In Scotland, there are eight police forces, each of which has a Police Authority or joint board. Police Authorities were arranged to match the old regional councils which were abolished in 1994. Only Fife and Dumfries and Galloway councils have their own Police Authority; the others have joint boards. As it was decided not to reorganise the police into smaller units, most police authorities in Scotland are run by joint boards across several local councils.

The Police Authority is the vehicle for ensuring that the police are accountable to the public. The police cannot do their job without the support of the general public. For example, the RUC in Northern Ireland has been abolished as part of the Good Friday peace agreement. It lost the support of a significant part of the community. A police authority is a committee made up of local councillors, independent members and local magistrates. It is their duty to maintain an 'efficient and effective' police force for their area. The police authority has three main duties:

1 To consult with the public and publish an annual Policing Plan. The Policing Plan looks at how each individual force is meeting the targets set nationally by the Scottish Executive, and how it is acting on issues of concern within the local area. The Chief Constable of a police force has responsibility for practical, operational matters.

2 To set a budget for the force and provide the Chief Constable with the resources required to effectively police the area.

3 To appoint senior ranks within the police (Assistant Chief Constable and above).

THE SCOTTISH EXECUTIVE

Within the Scottish Executive, the Minister for Justice and Home Affairs has primary responsibility for the police.

A powerful committee has been set up by the Scottish Parliament to advise the Minister. The Justice and Home Affairs Committee consults with, amongst others, the Police Advisory Board for Scotland. This is made up of representatives of the eight police authorities, chief constables, police staff organisations and 56 other appointed persons who have an expert knowledge of policing issues. The Minister will issue guidance, but each police authority has a strong degree of freedom in how it meets the national priorities and how it sets its own local priorities.

POLICE FINANCE

Both the Scottish Parliament and local authorities finance the police. Local government receives money from the Scottish Parliament and it will give a certain amount of this to the police force in its area. It will also give finance raised by council tax. Money for the police, therefore, ultimately, comes from the taxpayer. This is another reason why the police's actions have to be open and accountable to the public.

RANKS WITHIN THE POLICE

There is a promotion ladder within the police force. This reflects the level of responsibility each rank has.

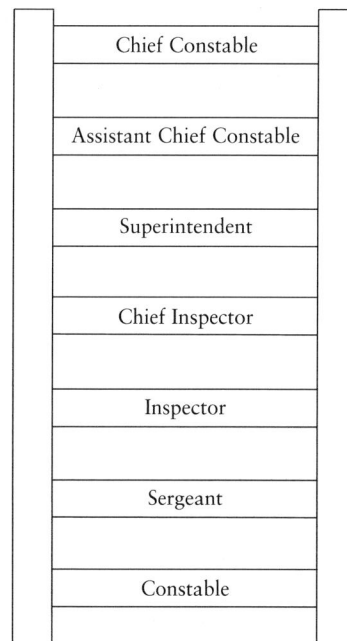

Chief Constable

Assistant Chief Constable

Superintendent

Chief Inspector

Inspector

Sergeant

Constable

POLICE STRATEGY

It is the police's job to protect the public. There are several strategies the police can use to do this.

Zero Tolerance

In 1998, Prime Minister Tony Blair announced that there would be a *"blitz on crime"*. Based on methods tried out in New York City, the Government identified 25 cities across the UK, including Glasgow, Edinburgh, London and Bristol, where certain crimes such as burglary and car theft are highest. Zero Tolerance policing means

---

INVESTIGATION

Case study of your police force.

Write a report on the police force in your area. Your report should have headings on each separate page.

1 Name of police force
2 Size and area of the force
3 Profile of the Chief Constable
4 Duties and members of the Police Authority
5 Crime in the area
6 Targets of the current policing plan
7 Conclusions: Success or problems of your police force.

Possible resources:
◆ *Social Issues in the UK* textbook
◆ BBC Scotland audiotape *Crime and the Law in Society*
◆ BBC Scotland video *Crime and the Law in Society*
◆ www.scottishpolice.uk

that computer software can analyse crime hotspots on a street by street basis. The police will then move into the area in large numbers and police it very strictly. Police will not move around in random or routine patrols, but will target known 'troublespots' and known 'troublemakers'.

There are certain situations where crime investigation is best served by the police not making themselves recognisable. Police officers may be involved in surveillance tasks which may involve disguising themselves as members of the public. Some high profile success has been achieved in breaking drugs smuggling gangs by officers involved in the 'deep' cover of infiltrating gangs, often at great personal risk, over a long period of time.

Already Zero Tolerance has had some success. Burglaries in Huddersfield are down 30% and those in Stockport by 21%. The most spectacular example has been the cleaning up of the area around Kings Cross station in London. This used to be an area notorious for prostitution. A Zero Tolerance approach, nicknamed 'Operation Welwyn', has successfully ended prostitution and the area has become a desirable place to live and work. Arsenal Football Club have made enquiries about moving to Kings Cross from their present base following good reports about the decrease in crime. Similarly, Tayside Police have achieved success with a 'focussed campaign, targeting known criminals'. Serious recorded crime was down 5.36% and property crimes were down by over 7%.

In 1997, Strathclyde Police set up 'The Spotlight Initiative'. While the term Zero Tolerance was not used, the aim was clear. If so-called nuisance or 'low level' crimes, such as vandalism, under-age drinking and disorder, could be tackled, more serious crimes such as assault could be prevented. The Spotlight Initiative was not just about Zero Tolerance. Adverts were placed on television and in newspapers warning of 'swoops' on offensive weapons. The public was informed of free, confidential phone lines to inform the police of known public nuisances.

Community policing

Community policing is seen to be an effective form of crime prevention and detection. The police will play an active role in the local community either by walking the streets ('beat policing') or by taking part in local initiatives such as neighbourhood watches and visits to schools. Crime can be prevented by citizens knowing the police on first name terms. Racial problems can be reduced if the police are actually recruited from the community in which it serves. Police forces have made strong efforts to attract officers from ethnic communities and to encourage the reporting of racially motivated crime.

After the urban riots of the 1980s in London, Liverpool and Birmingham, there was a deliberate move to 'return' to beat policing. It was claimed that the police had become remote from the local community, dealing with members of the public only when there was trouble. Driving around in cars or based in stations, the police were accused of 'harassing' suspects. Community policing reduces allegations of harassment because the police are more active in the community and are more likely to be aware of law abiding and criminal behaviour on a personal basis.

The growth of neighbourhood watch schemes has shown the success of community policing. Police perform educational roles in alerting the public to measures that prevent burglary and car crime. Leaflets are made available to the public to help educate them about the practical ways in which criminals can be deterred from committing crimes. Links can also be made between the public and the police through Neighbourhood Watch groups.

Proactive policing

Zero Tolerance policing has its critics. Some say that it can work well, but only for a short time. The problem, in the case of prostitution, may simply be shifted to another part of town. Harassing 'known criminals' may lead to resentment and tensions between the police and community, which could resurface in inner city riots. On the other hand, the statistics in reducing crimes are impressive. Beat or community policing is expensive, too. In reality, the police are likely to use a variety of strategies to stop crime, depending on the local circumstances. Such a strategy can be described as 'proactive policing'. Forces are likely to employ all of the above strategies at any one time, keeping the criminal guessing. The key to proactive policing is to be one step ahead of the criminal. This may be by crime prevention. It may also be by 'softly softly' community policing. Intelligence gathering by plain clothes officers is also vital. Computers are increasingly being used in gathering intelligence. Ultimately, police may use tougher 'hairy-chested' techniques, such as stop and search of 'known criminals' to deter them from committing crimes.

ACTIVITIES

1 What is meant by 'Zero Tolerance' policing? Give an example.
2 What are the main differences between Zero Tolerance and community policing?
3 Assess the advantages and disadvantages of Zero Tolerance and community policing.
4 What is meant by proactive policing? Why might police forces use a variety of different strategies?
5 Try to find examples of the type of strategy your police force is using at the moment.

POLICE ORGANISATION

Police forces in Scotland are usually split into three separate branches: Uniformed, Criminal Investigation and Traffic.

Uniformed Police

This is the type of police officer most of the public will come into contact with. Community Involvement policing has been the tradition in Scotland. In recent years, the police has adapted itself to set up multi-agency links with professionals, such as social workers and community workers, to foster good relations on deprived housing estates or areas where ethnic minority groups are concentrated.

Criminal Investigation Department (CID)

CID officers will usually work on a plain clothes basis. Becoming a CID officer is a form of promotion. Within the CID, officers can specialise in a particular aspect of crime. Most CIDs will now have a specialist drugs unit.

Traffic Police

Officers in the Traffic Police have to be skilled drivers who have attended special driving courses at the Scottish Police College at Tulliallan, Fife. It is the job of the Traffic Department to enforce speed restrictions and deal with accidents and emergencies on the roads.

POLICE RIGHTS AND RESPONSIBILITIES

The police in Scotland have the right to arrest someone without a warrant, if the police believe they have committed, or are about to commit, a crime. Likewise, the police have the power to enter a person's home without a warrant if they have reasonable reasons for believing a crime has been committed. The police also have the power to stop and search if it is believed that the person is carrying a weapon in a public place. Someone suspected of an imprisonable offence may be asked to 'help police with their enquiries' at a police station for up to six hours without charge. If arrested, however, suspects must be charged and the matter referred to the Procurator Fiscal. Interviews with the police are usually tape recorded to protect both parties.

The police in the UK are not armed, but most forces have specialist armed officers who can be made available should the need arise. In Northern Ireland, police officers can carry firearms.

Members of the public can make complaints about the police. In Scotland, complaints about police officers can be made to the Procurator Fiscal. Normally complaints are made directly to the police force, but this does not have to happen. The Procurator Fiscal is entirely independent of the police and has the power to investigate a complaint. A police officer can be disciplined if found to have acted in an unprofessional or criminal manner.

THE COURT SYSTEM IN SCOTLAND

Scots law is very different from English law. Scots law is based more on the legal principles and rules of ancient Rome than of England. As such, the Scottish court system is very different from that of England and Wales.

Action within the Criminal Justice System, 1997

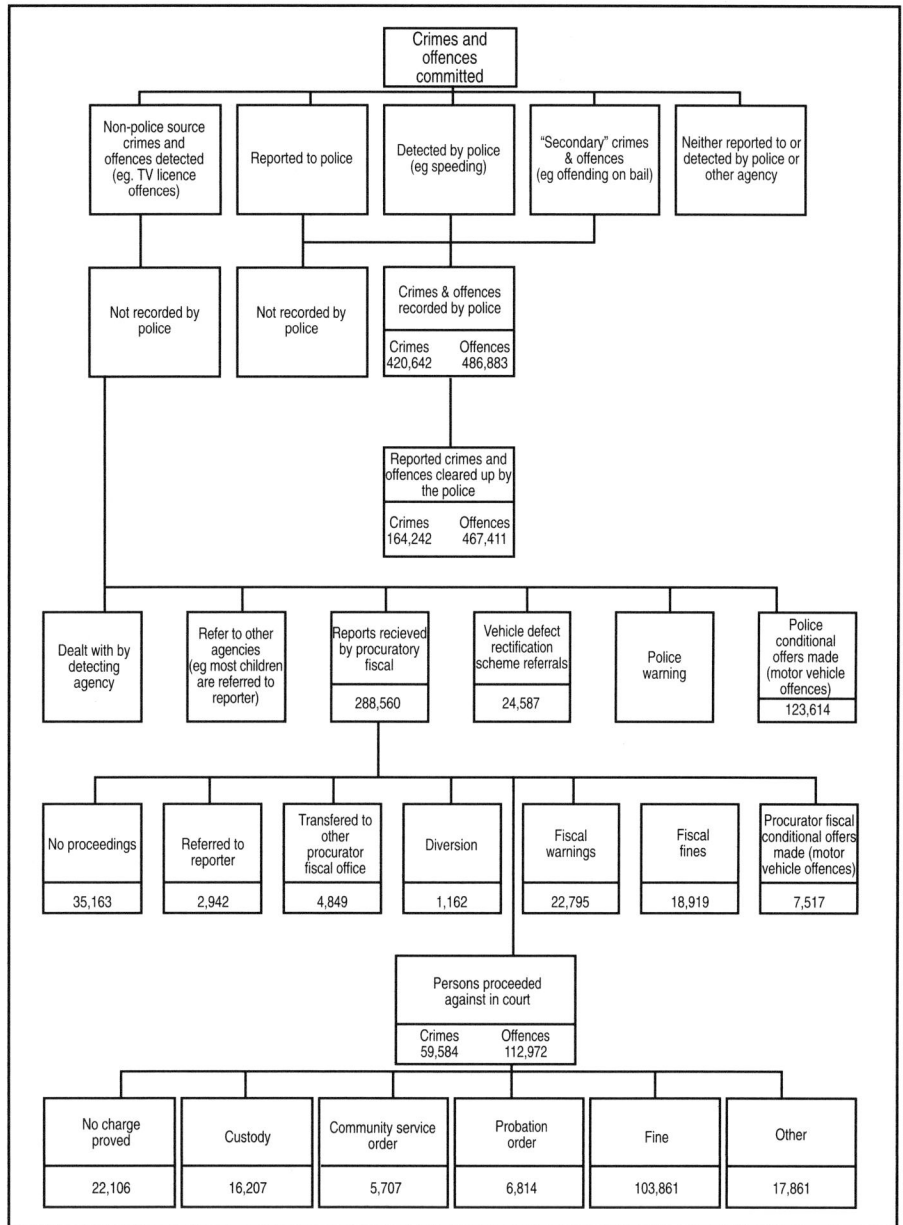

```
                          Crimes and
                           offences
                          committed
```

Non-police source crimes and offences detected (eg. TV licence offences)	Reported to police	Detected by police (eg speeding)	"Secondary" crimes & offences (eg offending on bail)	Neither reported to or detected by police or other agency

Not recorded by police	Not recorded by police	Crimes & offences recorded by police

Crimes & offences recorded by police

Crimes	Offences
420,642	486,883

Reported crimes and offences cleared up by the police

Crimes	Offences
164,242	467,411

Dealt with by detecting agency	Refer to other agencies (eg most children are referred to reporter)	Reports recieved by procuratory fiscal	Vehicle defect rectification scheme referrals	Police warning	Police conditional offers made (motor vehicle offences)
		288,560	24,587		123,614

No proceedings	Referred to reporter	Transfered to other procurator fiscal office	Diversion	Fiscal warnings	Fiscal fines	Procurator fiscal conditional offers made (motor vehicle offences)
35,163	2,942	4,849	1,162	22,795	18,919	7,517

Persons proceeded against in court

Crimes	Offences
59,584	112,972

No charge proved	Custody	Community service order	Probation order	Fine	Other
22,106	16,207	5,707	6,814	103,861	17,861

From prosecution to trial

When arrested, an accused person in Scotland may be held by the police in custody, or released to await a summons to appear in court. This would depend on the seriousness of the crime and whether the person was seen to be a danger to the public. In a serious case, the person would appear in court the next day, and would either be in kept in custody until trial, or released on bail. If released on bail, the accused must promise not to interfere with witnesses. The court may also insist that the accused stay away from certain people or places. Bail will not be granted if the accused is charged with murder, culpable homicide, rape or attempted rape or has any previous conviction for any of these crimes.

THE STRUCTURE OF THE COURT SYSTEM

The Lord Advocate and the Procurator Fiscal

In Scotland it is not the police who decide whether an accused will face trial, but the Lord Advocate. The Lord Advocate is the principal Law Officer for the Crown in Scotland. Private prosecutions in a criminal court by one individual against another are possible, but extremely rare. The Lord Advocate has a Crown Office, run by a Crown Agent, who is head of the Procurator Fiscal Service. There are local Procurators Fiscal in all areas of Scotland. In England and Wales, the decision to bring a case to court is made by the Crown Prosecution Service (CPS). In Scotland, the decision to prosecute or not is made by the Lord Advocate through the Procurator Fiscal (PF). In almost all cases, if a crime is reported to the PF by the police, a prosecution will lead to a court appearance. Unlike England and Wales, there is no Coroner in Scotland. If there is a suspicious death, the PF may report the case to the Crown Office. If a death arises in custody or there is death resulting from an industrial accident, a Fatal Accident Inquiry has to be set up.

Civil courts

Most civil cases, such as divorce, debt or custody battles over children, are heard in the Sheriff Court. Sometimes a very serious case can go direct to the Court of Session, based in Edinburgh. This is the supreme civil court in Scotland. The Court of Session will deal with cases involving disputes between individuals/organisations such as those involving complex compensation claims or damages. It has an Inner House and an Outer House. The Inner House is mainly an appeal court.

Criminal courts

There are three types of criminal courts in Scotland: the High Court of Judiciary, the Sheriff Court and the District Court. A criminal case will be heard in one of these courts, depending on the seriousness of the crime. The least serious crimes, such as petty shoplifting, may be heard in a local district court. The most serious crimes, e.g. murder, will be heard in the High Court.

The High Court of Judiciary

This is the most powerful criminal court in Scotland. It tries the most serious crimes such as murder, treason and rape. There are High Courts in Glasgow and Edinburgh.

The Sheriff Courts

There are a total of 49 sheriff courts in Scotland. If the case is tried under 'solemn procedure' i.e. with a jury, a sheriff may impose a prison sentence of up to three years and unlimited fine. If new evidence comes to light that makes the case more serious, the sheriff can refer the case to the High Court, where punishments are more severe.

The District Court

This court deals with minor offences. Most towns in Scotland have a District Court. The longest prison sentence that can be given is 60 days and the maximum fine is £2500.

Solemn procedure

This will take place in both the High Court and the Sheriff Court. A judge will sit with a jury of 15 members of the public. The Crown (prosecution) will set out its case, called an Indictment. The defence will offer a plea of 'Guilty' or 'Not Guilty'. The judge will decide questions of law and the jury has to decide on the facts of the case. A simple majority of the jury is sufficient to reach a verdict. It is up to the Crown to prove that the accused is guilty, as the accused is innocent until proven guilty. If a defendant has pleaded 'Not Guilty' but is found 'Guilty', a punishment will almost certainly be more severe. If the Crown cannot prove guilt, juries in Scotland have a choice of verdicts.

Juries in England and Wales have a straight choice between reaching a verdict of 'Guilty' or 'Not Guilty'. Scotland has the unique 'Three verdict system'. For a jury to return a verdict of 'Guilty', eight members must be clear beyond all reasonable doubt that this is the case. If they are not so satisfied, they can return either a 'Not Guilty' or a 'Not Proven' verdict. The last two verdicts are acquittals, meaning that the accused cannot be tried again for the same offence. Note that the word 'innocent' is not used in either verdict. Legally, the Crown has not proved that the accused is guilty. 'Innocence' is always a matter of opinion.

BETWEEN INNOCENCE AND GUILT – "THAT BASTARD VERDICT"

The Not Proven verdict is very controversial. It only exists in Scotland. It means that a jury cannot decide with complete certainty that a person is guilty. It may believe that the person is guilty but does not feel 'beyond all reasonable doubt' that this is so. A Not Proven verdict therefore does not carry the same weight of innocence as a Not Guilty verdict.

Neither innocent nor guilty, the Not Proven verdict was famously described by Sir Walter Scott as the "bastard verdict". It has existed in Scots law for over 300 years and has always been controversial. To some, it is a fair compromise in an imperfect world where juries and defendants cannot always be trusted. To others, it makes a mockery of the criminal justice system, leaving neither party happy with the result. The murder of schoolgirl Amanda Duffy in May 1992 sparked a fierce debate over the future of the Not Proven verdict.

Amanda Duffy was savagely murdered on the evening of 30th May 1992. Her body was found in a car park in Hamilton. A popular and talented pupil, she had been celebrating with friends her invitation for an interview for the Royal School of Music and Drama. Strong forensic evidence pointed to Mr Francis Auld as the killer. He had bitten her that evening, causing her intense pain and bleeding. Particles of his clothing were found near Amanda's body. The case against Mr Auld, heard before a High Court jury in November 1992, was found to be Not Proven. Auld had subsequently threatened a local man, Patrick Vandeleur, saying *"Patrick, you thought Amanda was the last – you're next"*.

Amanda's parents were so distraught at the verdict that they successfully took out a private prosecution against Francis Auld at the Court of Session. This was a civil action in a murder case – a very unusual occurrence. Joe and Kate Duffy sued Francis Auld for £50 000 as compensation for the 'loss to society' of their daughter. Francis Auld did not contest the claim and was ordered by the Court to pay the Duffy family £50 000. Mr Duffy concluded that *"it seems ironic that a criminal court with a jury of 15 people can acquit someone charged with the murder of our daughter, yet we can successfully raise a civil action. It makes a mockery of our legal system"*.

The Amanda Duffy case brought fresh calls for the abolition of the Not Proven verdict. The then local MP for Hamilton, George Robertson, supported the Duffys and helped in a campaign against the 'bastard verdict'. 60 000 signatures were raised in a public petition.

A famous debate was organised by *The Herald* newspaper at Glasgow University. Donald Findlay QC spoke for the Not Proven verdict. Donald Dewar, also a QC, spoke against the motion. It was a gripping debate, with both sides arguing convincing and emotional cases.

The Abolish Not Proven campaign finally managed to secure a vote in the House of Commons. A motion to abolish the verdict was

Donald Findlay (left), supported the Not Proven verdict. Donald Dewar (right), opposed it.

heard during debate of the Criminal Justice Bill (Scotland) in June 1995. It was defeated by 325 votes to 117.

Against the verdict

1 The 'Not Proven' verdict is a 'cop-out'. It is neither guilty nor not guilty. It allows guilty people to get off the hook. The jury should take the time to debate and come to a proper decision.
2 The verdict leaves a stain on the accused forever. He or she will always be under suspicion e.g. 'he did it, but it couldn't be proved'. This is not fair to those who could have had a 'Not Guilty' verdict and is too fair on those a jury feels might be guilty, but will not be decisive in its judgement. It leaves no-one satisfied.
3 It creates confusion for everyone. What is needed is a straight answer, guilty or not guilty. Surely the 'Not Proven' verdict only makes life for juries even more difficult.

For the verdict

1 There may be some cases where there is a shadow of a doubt whether a person is guilty. It would be unfair to send someone to jail for life when there was some doubt over their guilt.
2 The 'Not Proven' verdict allows juries to let a person go free if they are not completely sure. It is the job of the Crown to prove guilt, not the jury. If there is still doubt, the person should be acquitted.
3 It strengthens the 'Not Guilty' verdict. As the jury had a choice to record a 'Not Proven' verdict but did not take it and found the accused 'Not Guilty', the accused should have a stronger claim of innocence.

Some commentators pointed out that instead of the 'Not Proven' verdict being abolished, it is the 'Not Guilty' verdict that should be abolished, as complete and irrefutable innocence is rare. If there are to be three verdicts, a clearer definition of the three verdicts should be made and a certificate of innocence be made available for those who are indeed found 'Not Guilty'.

PUNISHMENTS

Custodial punishments

In Scotland, a custodial sentence will mean jail for an adult, or a Young Offender's Institution for young people aged between 16 and 21.

A custodial sentence will only be given when it is considered that the offender poses a serious risk to the public. A judge may decide on a suspended sentence. This means that a prison sentence has been given, but the offender can walk free. If, however, they commit another offence during the suspended time, the prison sentence will be imposed.

ACTIVITIES

1 What is the difference between the verdicts open to Scottish and English courts in criminal cases?
2 Explain why the 'Not Proven' verdict has been described as "that bastard verdict".
3 Why is innocence a matter of opinion in criminal cases?
4 Describe why the Amanda Duffy case led to calls for the abolition of the 'Not Proven' verdict in Scotland.
5 Debate the motion *"This class believes that the Not Proven verdict pleases no-one"*.

Duncan Ferguson, jailed after breaking a suspended sentence

In 1995, Duncan Ferguson was given a suspended sentence after committing several violent assaults. He broke his suspended sentence when he headbutted a footballer during a game. A spectator at the match reported the incident to the Procurator Fiscal, who referred the matter to the Sheriff Court.

A life sentence will be given for murder, and is available for certain other offences. The offender may be released when it is considered by the First Minister that they no longer pose a risk to the public. The Sex Offenders Act requires those released from prison to inform police of their address. They are then placed on a register for life and monitored through a civil Community Protection Order.

Non-custodial punishments

The Scottish Executive has pledged to cut the number of custodial sentences, punishing people in the community, wherever possible. Fines are still the most common type of punishment imposed by courts. Alternatively, judges may impose a Probation Order. This means that an offender will have to report to a Probation Officer and take steps to amend their behaviour, such as applying for jobs or attending college. The offender can also be given a Community Service Order. This means that the individual must do a number of hours of work helping in the community. A caution simply means that the person has been warned not to appear before the court again. No other punishment is given, but if the offending continued, punishment would be more severe in future.

During 1999, the Scottish Executive gave permission for the introduction of electronic tagging. This means that a Curfew Order is placed on the offender. The police can monitor the offender's movements electronically and will always know where an offender is. The person may have orders to be indoors at certain times. This is much cheaper than prison and allows the person to reorganise their life while still being monitored.

Why seek alternatives to prison?

Prison has four main aims:

1 To punish the individual.
2 To protect the public.
3 To act as a deterrent to criminals.
4 To rehabilitate the offender (change their behaviour).

In recent years there has been a lot of evidence to suggest that custodial sentences were achieving the first two aims, but failing in the latter two. Custodial sentences were neither frightening criminals from committing crimes nor changing their behaviour.

The prospect of 'doing time' did not appear to frighten prisoners. Re-offending rates for those coming out of prison are high. Likewise, not enough offenders were changing for the good in prison. While some prisoners did reflect on their life and change for the better, for example by taking advantage of education programmes, some became tougher, more hardened criminals. Contacts were made in jail, which led to more criminal behaviour once released. Prisons were acting as 'universities of crime'. In recent years, it has been difficult to control drug taking and dealing. There have been a number of suicides in jail. Prison also is extremely expensive. It is estimated that it costs around £300 per week to keep an adult in jail.

These are the reasons why the Scottish Executive has urged judges not to send offenders to jail, unless they are a risk to the public.

ACTIVITIES

1   Draw a spider diagram showing the various punishments that are possible in the Scottish criminal justice system.
2   What are the main aims of prison?
3   In your opinion, are prisons succeeding in their declared aims? Give reasons for your answer.
4

Source A

"It is much better that non-violent offenders are punished in the community. Under community service, young offenders can be given a tough punishment. They have to meet their probation officer early in the morning and do valuable work in the community. They are forced to work hard and change their criminal behaviour. In the meantime, they can be given help from professionals as drugs are often the root of the problem. They are forced to look at themselves and change their life for the better. This is not a soft option."

Source B

"Punishment in the community is a joke. Car thieves and junkies these days must be laughing at the law. A prison sentence would give them a right good fright and teach them not to commit crimes again. Instead they get fussed over by do-gooding social workers who make excuses for them. No wonder there is so much crime these days. Villains are better looked after than many elderly people".
What are the differences between Source A and Source B in their views on punishment in the community?
Which view do you agree with? Give reasons for your answer.

5   *"Custodial sentences are a waste of time and money"*. What evidence is there for and against this statement?
6   Why is the Scottish Executive keen to reduce the numbers of people receiving custodial sentences?

YOUNG OFFENDERS

Child crime in Scotland is on the increase. In 1993 there were 34 000 offences recorded. In 1998/99 this had increased to 42 000. In Scotland, criminal proceedings may be brought against any child aged 8 years or over. Only the Lord Advocate can give permission for anyone aged under 16 to be prosecuted. The law in Scotland holds parents responsible for the actions of their children until the age of 16. It is only in cases of murder or serious assault that a court prosecution is possible. In most cases of law breaking, children under the age of 16 are thought to be in need of care and protection, rather than prosecution. They will therefore be brought before a Children's Hearing.

THE CHILDREN'S HEARING

It is only relatively recently that children have been treated as children by the criminal justice system. Before the 20th century, children were punished in exactly the same ways as adults. Justice was geared solely towards punishing the individual rather than securing change in future behaviour.

The 1908 Children Act set up separate Juvenile Courts, but it was only in England and Wales that these courts became widely established. In 1962 in Scotland, only four burghs were running juvenile courts. The majority of children's cases were being held in adult sheriff or burgh (later, district) courts. The **Kilbrandon Committee** changed this and decided that special Children's Panels should be set up. It felt that the wrong-doings of children should be treated differently from those of adults. It was important that justice for children should be the same all over Scotland. Likewise, as 95% of children were admitting guilt in courts, there was no need for the trials and tribulations of court action. Kilbrandon wanted the new panel system to be *educational*. The members of panels should be people who 'know about children, rather than know about the law'. Children's Panels were first set up in 1971. Only the name has significantly changed, to the less threatening **Children's Hearing**.

How the Children's Hearing works

The first point of contact is the Reporter. The police, education department, social worker or indeed any concerned member of the public can consult the Reporter to the Children's Hearing and request that a particular child be brought before a Hearing. The Reporter will investigate the case and make a decision whether or not to proceed. The Reporter will ask the parents if a child can appear before a Children's Hearing. If parental permission is not given, a Sheriff can decide whether the child should appear or not.

The **Children (Scotland) Act 1995** has set out the reasons why a child may appear before a Children's Hearing. These may be because the child is:

1 beyond the control of parents
2 exposed to moral danger
3 likely to suffer through parental neglect
4 the victim of physical injury or sexual abuse
5 failing to attend school
6 indulging in solvent abuse

7 misusing drugs and/or alcohol

8 involved in breaking the law

Children's Hearings in Scotland are very different from courtrooms. There is an informal atmosphere, designed to put the young person at ease and to allow an honest discussion of the problems facing the child. Discussion takes place around a table. Those on the Hearing are not judges, but ordinary members of the public. They do not wear gowns or wigs; they dress smartly, but casually. Their aim is to help, not punish the child. Only those who can prove an interest and can communicate well with children will be allowed to take part in a Hearing. There is no need for formal qualifications. A Hearing consists of three Panel members, and will also include the child with their parents, a social worker and other professionals. The child can also bring along a friend.

Measures the Hearing can take

Often the very fact that the Hearing takes place can help the child. This may be the first chance they have to speak about their problems in a non-threatening environment. The Hearing is there to consider what is in the best interests of the child and it will only recommend a course of action which it feels will help.

The Hearing will receive reports from school and the social work department. It does not have the power to fine a child or the parents. There are three courses of action open to the Hearing.

- Firstly, it could decide that the original problem has gone away and that no action is required.
- Secondly, it could decide to place a **Supervision Requirement**, which may be renewed until the child becomes 18. This would happen if the Hearing feels that it is best that the child stays in the parental home, but requires extra supervision. A Supervision Requirement means that a social worker will visit the family from time to time to make sure the problems are going away.
- Alternatively, the Hearing may decide that it is in the best interests of the child to move them away from the home environment. In this case, the child may be put under the care of foster parents, a children's home or a residential school.

All decisions made by the Hearing are legally binding on the child. The child or parents may appeal against the decision to the Sheriff, but this must be done within 21 days.

The system is widely seen to be superior to the old court system, but not everyone is always pleased with the Hearing. The following opinions are taken from a major conference on Children's Hearings organised by *Barnardo's*. Attending the conference were teenagers, parents, members of the Children's Hearings, Reporters to the Children's Hearings, teachers and social workers.

Social work reports

"Why do they use so many big long words."

Teenager

ACTIVITIES

1 Give three reasons why the Kilbrandon Committee wanted Children's Panels to be set up.

2 Describe the process of how a child appears before a Children's Hearing. Show this in a diagram.

3 Give three examples of situations where a child would be asked to appear before a Hearing.

4 Describe three differences between a Children's Hearing and a courtroom.

5 What are the three courses of action open to the Children's Hearing?

"Whose report is it? Does the social worker see it as his? I was told it's the Reporter's because he asks the social work department to write it for him. What I think is that if it's saying things about me and my family, it is sort of mine. So surely I should be entitled to see it what's in it"?

Parent

"The first Hearing I went to was alright. You know why? Because I knew what was in the report. But see the next one, it was dreadful because I didn't know what they were saying about me and I knew my mum would be there and she thinks I just tell lies all the time."

Teenager

Atmosphere during a Hearing

"I think there should be a kind of helpline for kids, not run by adults but by kids who've already been to a Panel. Because if you've been to a Panel you know what to tell people who've never been before."

Teenager

"I don't know why they make you introduce the people around the table. It made me feel stupid – like a wee kid."

Teenager

"When you're uptight, what you say can come out completely wrong."

Parent

"They wanted me to talk about my mother but she was sitting there right beside me. How could I do that? It was so embarrassing."

Teenager

Membership of the Hearing

"Panel members don't feel like ordinary folk. They sound like snobs."

Teenager

"Panel members can be dead crabbit, but some of them are dead nice."

Teenager

The Hearing system

"The Panel's better than the court. It's better being able to take your time and talk."
"The court's easier than the Panel because the lawyer speaks for you."
"I know the best Hearing I went to was the one when I took my boyfriend along. He was a great support and it made the panel treat me much more like an adult."
"Your best Hearing's your last isn't it?"

Teenagers

The conclusions by all the participants at the conference were that they were happy with the principle of Children's Hearings but that a number of improvements could be made to the workings of them. The main recommendations were:

Before the Hearing

- There should be better leaflets, explaining how Hearings work and making it clear that a child can bring a friend along.
- Someone should be able to help the child write their own report.
- Children and parents should see the report days in advance of the Hearing.
- There should be more information made available on how to get in touch with the Reporter.
- Children should learn more about their rights at school.
- Children should be told clearly in language they can understand why they have to appear at a Hearing.

At the Hearing

- The Hearing should stop asking children to introduce people.
- The members should say a bit more about themselves.
- Jargon words should not be used.
- If possible, children should get Hearing members they know.
- There should be a break in the middle, to allow children time to think.

Hearing member's training

Hearing members should:
- Spend some time working in a children's home.
- Know more about the European Convention on the Rights of the Child.
- Visit the area where the child lives.

Role play

Read over pages 110–112 on 'How the Children's Hearing System works'. Each person in the group should be given a role, and a script should be prepared. The room should be organised as far as possible in the way a Hearing would be. The Social Worker should prepare a report on the case. The child should be able to write a report too. Before the Hearing, distribute the report. Have your hearing in class. At the end, the members of the Hearing must decide to take either of the three forms of action open to it.

YOUNG OFFENDERS INSTITUTIONS

There are four Young Offenders Institutions in Scotland: Cornton Vale in Stirling, Dumfries, Glenochil in Tullibody, and Polmont near Falkirk. Young Offenders aged over 16 will be sent to one of these institutions if the judge feels that the young person is a danger to the community. A balance between **punishment** and 'rehabilitation' (the

---

INVESTIGATION

Title: *The Children's Hearing system has greatly improved the justice system for children, but it is not perfect.*

Write up your answer to each heading on a separate piece of paper.

1 Weaknesses of the system before the Kilbrandon Report.
2 How the Children's Hearing system works.
3 Why children appear before a Children's Hearing.
4 The atmosphere of a Children's Hearing.
5 Criticisms of the Hearing system.
6 Ways in which the Hearing system could be improved.
7 Conclusion – sum up your answer to the statement in the title.

changing of behaviour) is aimed for. The institutions are subject to regular inspections. It is clear that while the staff work hard to help the young people, these remain establishments to be avoided! Perhaps this is an unwritten aim!

HM Young Offender's Institution, Polmont

Inspected:	May 1998
Accommodation:	Based in Brighton, near Falkirk. Seven halls; YOs based in dormitories and single/double cells. Toilet in cells by 'porta-potties' emptied every day.
Population:	Designed for 452, but held 473. One 'Life' prisoner. Two doing 10-year sentences. The majority of YOs serving sentences between 6 months and 2 years.
Routine:	0645h Morning check
	0800h Breakfast
	0830h Work
	1200h Lunch
	1230h Lock-up
	1300h Work
	1630h Lock-up
	1700h Evening meal
	1745h Lock-up
	1900h Evening recreation
	2100h Lock-up
Issues:	Problems of 'tribalism', bullying and fighting. Evidence of illegal drug misuse. 50 Young Offenders had been involved in fighting in the past year with 15 YOs and four staff injured. There had been only one suicide in the past five years but many cases of self-harm. Authoritarian relationship between staff and YOs. Staff address YOs by last name only.
Good points:	Good catering, PE and health facilities.

ACTIVITY

Extended writing

"Being sent to a Young Offender's Institution would be a life-changing experience".
Refer to Polmont YOI. Your essay should mention possible bullying/violence/loss of freedom and the lack of luxuries

THE YOUTH SYSTEM IN ENGLAND AND WALES

England and Wales do not have a system of Children's Hearings. Instead, there are separate Youth Courts. Children between the ages of 10 and 18 can appear at a Youth Court. Only the most serious crimes will go before a full criminal court. Proceedings take place in private.

In England and Wales, the Labour Government has embarked on a bold review of the youth justice system. Under the Crime and Disorder Act 1998, it seeks to put crime prevention as the principal aim of the youth justice system. It gives local authorities, the police and the courts new powers to try to prevent crime, and new punishments if it happens.

Crime prevention

- *Child curfews*. Local authorities can apply to the Home Office for powers to make sure that children under the age of 10 must be at home after certain hours, usually 9pm.
- *Anti-social behaviour orders* to deal with serious, but not necessarily criminal, anti-social behaviour by those aged 10 and above.
- *Action on truanting*. If the police catch a young person truanting, the force now has the power to take the child to a 'secure establishment'.

Punishment

- *A final warning scheme*. This replaces the police cautioning of young offenders.
- *Reparation Order*. This requires young offenders to make amends to the victims of their crime.
- *Parenting Order*.

The Government aims to speed up the process from arrest to sentencing in the Youth Courts. The ultimate aim is to get Youth Offenders into court the day after a charge is made.

At a national level, the new Youth Justice Board for England and Wales began operation in September 1998. This oversees the work of the new Youth Offending Teams which work at a local level. Youth Offending Teams are multi-agency organisations and are composed of police, social workers, probation service, education workers and health workers. They have a legal responsibility to set targets to reduce youth crime in their area.

There is a clear difference between the Scottish system and that which exists in England and Wales. In the first place, in England and Wales, all young people over the age of 10 are treated the same. While offenders appear in a Youth Court, rather than a criminal court, once crime prevention has failed, the emphasis is on punishment at a far earlier age than in Scotland. A new aspect of the English system, which appears to have built on the Scottish system, is the new initiative on **Early Intervention**. Under this new system, if a first time young offender pleads guilty and does not require a custodial sentence, a Referral Order will be made to a 'panel drawn from the community'. The reasons for offending will be examined and a contract will be drawn up between panel members, the Youth Offending Team, the young person and their parents. The panel arrangements were first piloted in 2000.

Why do young people offend?

The children's pressure group Article 12 (www.article12.org) carried out a survey of young people in towns and cities across Scotland. The most common reason given for youth crime was "boredom", "nothing to do". This echoed the more extensive research carried

ACTIVITIES

1 What are the main differences between the English and Scottish systems of dealing with Young Offenders?
2 What similarities are there between the Scottish Children's Hearing System and the English Early Intervention System?

out by the Scottish Office in 1995. It found that the main reasons for offending were:

◆ poor parental management
◆ low intelligence
◆ a deprived background.

The above factors tend to coincide with each other.

It found that a large proportion of the crime was carried out by a small number of young people, showing that the vast majority of teenagers were not involved in any criminal acts.

ACTIVITIES

What can be done? In groups, discuss what you think should be done to help young people stay out of crime.

First, brainstorm the problems and then suggest possible solutions. Think of the rights that you should have, but also your responsibilities. You should consider what the following can do to help:

◆ young people themselves
◆ parents, schools and community groups
◆ local councils
◆ the Scottish Parliament.

One member of the group should report back to the class.

It is important to remember that solutions cost money. You must state where the money for your proposals could come from, who would benefit and why. Why would your ideas work where other ones have failed?

CRIMES INVOLVING CARS AND DRUGS

CAR CRIME

The Autoglass car crime league table, 1999

1 Greater London
2 Manchester
3 Birmingham
4 Glasgow
5 Newcastle/Gateshead

Strathclyde Police's Spotlight Initiative places a strong emphasis on cutting car crime. Glasgow is the fourth most likely place in the UK to suffer car crime. Edinburgh was in 18th place with Bothwell, South Lanarkshire, closely behind. During the year 1998/99 a car crime was reported to Strathclyde Police every 11 minutes. Most offenders were between 16 and 18 years of age and typically had an average of 26 previous convictions.

Car crime is a very serious crime for several reasons.

Four boys were killed in this collision, joyriding in April 1999

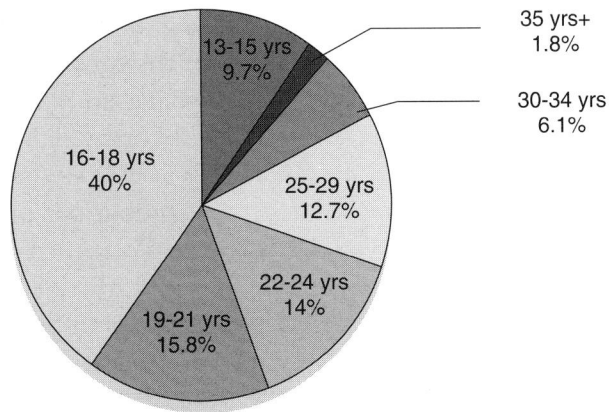

Car crime rates according to age (Source: The Herald)

♦ Firstly, those stealing cars pose a threat to their own lives and those of other members of the public. So-called 'joyriders' are more likely to drive in a dangerous manner than other road users. The main speeding offenders were young male drivers between the ages of 17 and 25. This age group accounts for 20% of all accidents, despite only holding 10% of all licences. In Scotland, 16 young drivers are involved in an accident every day. One is killed every week; 17 are seriously injured. These so-called 'boy racers' are more likely to drive dangerously and without care and attention than other road users. Several high profile crashes involving young men occurred in 1999. The most common reason given for speeding was the need to 'impress' their friends. Courts often hear stories about how defendants are 'obsessed' with cars.

♦ Secondly, those who have their cars stolen or broken into are put under great inconvenience. The owner has the option of claiming the loss under their insurance policy, in which case the cost will go up the following year. The alternative is to pay directly for the damage. In both cases, the innocent party is out of pocket, even if the criminal is caught. It is estimated that car crime in Strathclyde alone cost £76m in 1999 in direct damages to property. This was not counting the costs of police officers, court cases, social workers, prisons and raised insurance premiums.

♦ Thirdly, there is a strong connection between car crime and the drugs trade. At one level, money raised from the sale of stolen cars goes on drugs. Lower down the criminal scale, possessions are often stolen from cars for resale to finance a person's drug habit. One in five people convicted of car crime has a previous conviction for drug offences.

In 1998, 23% of cars stolen in Strathclyde were never recovered. Instead they were possibly 'chopped' by professional car criminals. This involves breaking cars up and rebuilding the parts into 'new' cars. In one raid on garage premises, police recovered eight stolen vehicles worth about £100 000. In Paisley, a man appeared in court after the theft of a bus valued at £50 000. So-called 'cutting and shutting' is one of the most lucrative vehicle crimes around. It is also one of the most dangerous. Not only is the unsuspecting buyer purchasing an illegal vehicle, it will be extremely unsafe and unroadworthy. Chopped vehicles have been described as 'coffins on wheels'.

To combat car crime, Strathclyde Police have used a combination of Zero Tolerance and re-education techniques.

In 1999, the Zero Tolerance initiative was extended to all eight police forces in Scotland in an effort to cut car crime. The three month **Operation Impact** emphasised:

♦ putting police resources into crime 'hotspots' using computer-aided analysis
♦ placing random road blocks in hotspot areas
♦ using satellite tracking to locate stolen vehicles
♦ using DNA swabbing of suspected drug and car crime offenders to see if they are linked to other crimes
♦ using advertising campaigns on car security on radio, posters and parking meters
♦ highlighting Crimestoppers 0800 555 111 as a confidential, freephone service to report crime
♦ organising raids on 'chopping shops'

Alongside the Zero Tolerance strategy, Strathclyde Police set up a **Young Drivers Project**. This is known as a police academy for young drivers. Through talks and presentations, police officers try to improve the attitudes of young people towards safe driving. Glasgow Social Work Department also organised the Glasgow Motoring Project. As part of a probation programme, the emphasis is placed on re-educating repeat vehicle offenders. Those who attend the course have to consider the effect their crimes have on the victims of car crime and reflect on the damage their actions have caused. There have been many success stories. In 1999, of the 22 offenders who completed the project, only three had reoffended.

ACTIVITIES

"Most car criminals are teenagers who are looking to steal easy-to-carry objects for resale."

1 What evidence is there to support the above point of view?
2 *"The legal driving age for males should be increased to 21"*. Discuss the arguments for and against this point of view.
3 Which view do you agree with. Give reasons for your answer.
4 Carry out a survey of male/females in your class on attitudes to driving. Your hypothesis is *"males care more about driving fast than driving safely"*. Make up questions that will allow you to test whether your hypothesis is true or false. Show your findings in bar/pie charts and analyse your results.

5 Describe the efforts of Strathclyde Police to cut down on car crime.
6 What measures could a careful car buyer take to make sure that they did not purchase a 'chopped' car?

THE HAMILTON CHILD SAFETY INITIATIVE

In the town of Hamilton in central Scotland, any child under 16 who does not have a 'reasonable excuse' to be out at night is sent home by the police. It is part of the Zero Tolerance approach by Strathclyde Police, to stop 'neds' loitering in the streets and having the opportunity to commit crime. The 'Hamilton curfew' won a prize in the 1998 British Crime Prevention and Community Safety Awards. It has been suggested that the Hamilton curfew be copied throughout Scotland. Under the Crime and Disorder Act in England and Wales, local councils have the power to introduce a curfew.

There are arguments for and against the Child Safety Initiative for the under 16s.

For

1 It protects the elderly from gangs of youths who may roam around a particular area.
2 It protects young children from possible paedophiles who may be in the neighbourhood.
3 It protects children from peer group pressure to drink or take drugs.
4 It is supported by good parents who care where their children are at night, rather than allow them to 'hang around with mates'.
5 The under-16s can still be out after 9 o'clock, so long as they are taking part in organised activities i.e. at a friend's house or at a youth club. It is only those roaming the streets who must go home for their own safety.

Against

1 The curfew increases parents' worries that their child will get into trouble, only this time simply by being out too late.
2 Most under-16s are not involved in crime. Punishing all under-16s is unfair.
3 Parents can be labelled 'bad parents' unnecessarily.
4 The curfew encourages anxiety and prejudice against teenagers. People will assume that they are all criminals.

ACTIVITY

Extended writing
"The Child Safety Initiative has been a success in preventing crime."
Discuss this statement.

DRUG CRIME

A national survey carried out in Scotland in 1998 showed that drugs was the second most important issue facing Scots, coming before

SOCIAL ISSUES IN THE UK

issues such as housing, health and poverty. The organisation *Scotland Against Drugs* estimates that by the age of 13, most pupils in Scotland will have been offered drugs. By the age of 16, half will have experimented.

There are many drugs. Some, such as aspirin, are freely available over the supermarket counter. Others, such as cigarettes and alcohol, are controlled by age restriction, but are legal, and in varying social situations, are seen as acceptable. The Misuse of Drugs Act (1971) classifies illegal drugs into different categories. There are different punishments for the dealing and taking of these different drugs.

	Class A	Class B	Class C
Type of drug	Heroin, Acid, Ecstasy, Cocaine, Crack	Cannabis, Amphetamines	Some tranquilisers like Temazepam, anabolic steroids
Max. penalty for dealing	Life jail sentence and/or seizure of assets; fine	14 year jail sentence and/or seizure of assets; unlimited fine	Five year jail sentence and/or unlimited fine
Max. penalty for possession	Seven years and/or unlimited fine	five years and/or unlimited fine	Two years and/or fine

The police are careful to draw the difference between *dealers* and *users* of drugs. Dealers are dealt with much more severely. An individual in possession of a number of drugs will have to counter the charge that they were for resale rather than for their own personal use. The police are also keen to keep dealers and users apart in prison. In the past, dealers and users have been put in the same jail or Young Offenders Institution which has helped create a drug culture inside the institution, rather than help the user to become drug free.

The debate over the harm done by drug taking and the penalties imposed on those who supply and take drugs is a contentious one. There is little doubt that Class A drugs are harmful to health, and often kill. Heroin abuse can be found in towns and cities throughout the UK. In the space of two weeks in 1999, Strathclyde Police arrested 92 suspected criminals and seized drugs worth almost £2.2 million. Heroin is widely seen as a 'loser's drug'. There around 200 000 heroin addicts in the UK. All classes in society can suffer from drug abuse, but the problem is especially severe in deprived areas, where people feel a sense of hopelessness.

Living with the dragon

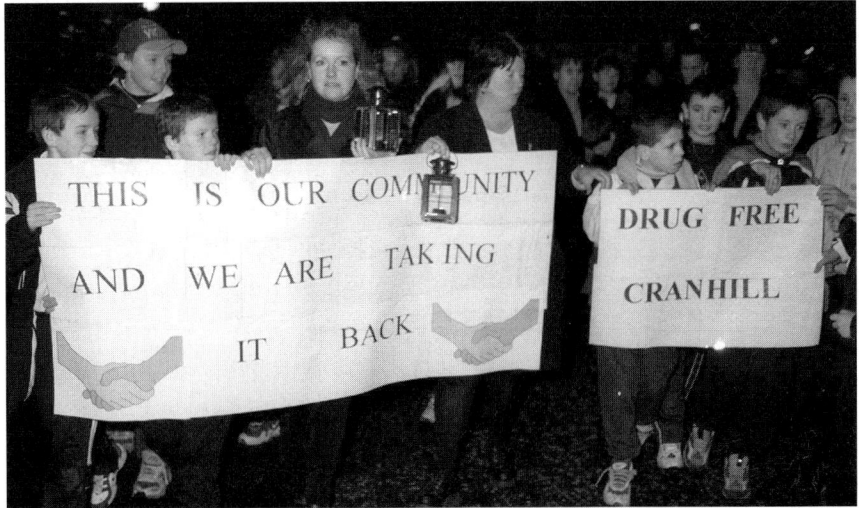

In January 1998, Allan Harper (13) from Cranhill, Glasgow, became Britain's youngest heroin victim.

In Cranhill, it is easier to get drugs than it is to get cigarettes from the ice cream van. It is easier to get a £10 bag of heroin than a fresh pint of milk from the local shop. The shops run out of milk, but the dealers never run out of heroin. This is a decaying housing scheme, a 15-minute bus ride from the cruel contrast that is Glasgow city centre. There is no colour and little brightness. It is an area starved of oxygen, whose very existence is a chronicle of contemporary decline. If Cranhill were a streetfight, it would be 50 stitches in the head and a bullet in the back of the head.

Glasgow was supposed to have left all the old ways behind: the drinking, the violence, the poor housing, the street gangs and the unemployment. In their place supposedly came the restaurants, the writers, the nightclubs and the wine bars – the City of Architecture and Design. Try telling that to a Cranhill local.

The good families, and there are many, have no desire to leave Cranhill but have been under enormous pressure since their young fell under the spell of heroin. Formed in the aftermath of revulsion that swept Cranhill after Allan died, the loudest voices are from Mothers Against Drugs (MAD).

Adapted from Living With the Dragon, *by Michael Tierney,* The Herald Magazine, *14 November 1998*

In 1999, the UK Government appointed a national co-ordinator, Keith Hellawell (the so-called 'drugs czar') to lead the fight against drugs. In Scotland, the all-party organisation *Scotland Against Drugs* was formed in 1996. It aims to make drug taking and dealing socially unacceptable. Until recent times, drunk driving was tolerated, even admired as 'macho'. There has been a change in attitudes towards drink driving, with most people now frowning on those who do it, and most motorists would now not consider drink driving. *Scotland Against Drugs* seeks to achieve the same change in attitudes among young people towards drugs.

"Our view on drugs is simple: If you are not experimenting with drugs then do not start, and if you are experimenting we would encourage you to stop and minimise the damage to yourself, your family and ultimately your community."

Scotland Against Drugs

While few in society believe that drugs are a source of good, there is debate as to how the drugs problem can be tackled. *Scotland Against Drugs* admits that the general message to all of "Just say No" has not been effective. Young people, especially vulnerable young people, can be naturally rebellious. The more someone in authority says "don't do it", the more attractive the "it" can be. There has been a debate over the best tactics and *Scotland Against Drugs* has become more focussed in its approach. Recent examples have been its advertising campaigns: *Paranoid Instamatic* was a television advert which was aimed at 13–16 year olds. *Rave* was aimed at 16–20 year olds and *Aggressive* was for older people tempted to experiment with drugs.

The latest adverts have been aimed at highlighting the differences in lives between those who choose drugs and those who choose to stay drug free. One teenage boy chooses drugs, loses his friends and gradually becomes more ill. He eventually becomes reduced to begging in the street. The other boy does well in school, is popular with friends and takes part in sport. Apart from emphasising the 'choose life' message, it aims to give confidence to non-users to offer advice to friends who are taking drugs.

The adverts are supported by posters, leaflets in magazines and resources and training given to teachers and community workers involved with young people. There is a recognition that sending one message to all young people is not enough. Some young people will never be tempted by drugs. Some will, but can be dissuaded by different arguments.

As the drugs problem in Scotland has escalated, *Scotland Against Drugs* has been criticised as being ineffective. There has been criticism that it is remote from the poorest communities that are most affected by drugs. In 1998, *Scotland Against Drugs* addressed this criticism and promised to work more closely with organisations such as the Cranhill *Mothers Against Drugs*.

The community-based *Calton Athletic* has adopted a 'cold turkey' approach to the heroin crisis in the poorest communities. Calton Athletic is a charity and a football team based in the East End of Glasgow. Only those who have become drug free can wear the famous Calton Athletic T-shirt. Calton Athletic believe that it is not poverty or lack of opportunity that leads young people to heroin but peer pressure to experiment. The answer, therefore, is to take the person away from the peer pressure. Calton Athletic does not believe in weaning the addict off drugs by use of substitutes such as methadone or diazapan. Rather it believes in total abstinence from drugs and a new healthy lifestyle. Through a fitness and health programme and by support from other ex-addicts, Calton Athletic believes this is the only long-term cure. Calton Athletic has had many successes. However, while the individual may well have been pressurised into taking drugs, the heroin crisis is at its worst in the poorest communities. There is a clear link between drugs and poverty. There has been no need for a Calton Athletic in affluent areas such as Bearsden in Glasgow or Morningside in Edinburgh.

In 1999, Tom Wood, Deputy Chief Constable of Lothian and Borders Police, called for a Scottish drugs czar to be appointed. While praising the efforts of the many organisations involved in fighting drugs, he felt that too many people across the country were not working together enough. In 1999, there were more than 130 anti-drug organisations, some of which do the same job, but others of which compete for scarce resources such as staff and facilities. A Scottish drugs czar could supervise the fight and also take responsibility for alcohol- and tobacco-related abuse.

ACTIVITIES

1   Describe the efforts of Scotland against Drugs (www.sad.org.uk) and Calton Athletic to combat drug abuse.
2   Give reasons for the increase in the use and supply of heroin in poor housing areas in recent years?
3   What does Tom Wood believe should be done to combat the drug problem?
4   What, in your opinion, would be effective ways to keep young people away from drugs?

Should cannabis be legalised?

Although a Class B drug, in recent years cannabis has become more socially acceptable. While reliable figures are difficult to obtain, it is estimated that over 6.3 million people in Britain have tried it. Several members of the Scottish Parliament have admitted taking the drug. Even a President of the United States, Bill Clinton, admitted taking cannabis as a student (although he claimed he did not 'inhale'!). The leader of the Liberal Democrats, Charles Kennedy, has called for a top level enquiry, called a **Royal Commission**, to examine whether cannabis should be legalised. There are strong arguments on both sides. You are the jury!

For

1   The medical use of cannabis can be traced back many years. The magazine *Disability Now* surveyed its readers and found that 25% of disabled people took the drug with their doctor's

approval. Sufferers of multiple sclerosis, in particular, claim that cannabis is a great pain reliever.

2 Unlike alcohol use, cannabis use, it is claimed, does not lead to violence. Cannabis use leads to a happy peaceful feeling, rather than the aggression and violence common with alcohol.

3 Cannabis is legal in other countries, such as Holland, and it has not been abused. Those who claim that there will be a flood of cannabis addicts also claimed that there would be more alcoholics when pubs were allowed to open all day in 1983. The result has been more civilised drinking. The same would be true of cannabis use.

4 It is claimed that cannabis is less harmful than other accepted substances such as alcohol or tobacco.

5 The legalisation of cannabis could result in great tax revenues for the Government. At the moment, profits from cannabis sales go into the pockets of drug dealers. Those profits could be used for the NHS or education.

6 The law at the moment is being ignored. If prisoners have had easy access to cannabis, most of the public could have access to it if they wanted. Some otherwise responsible law-abiding people have been given needless criminal records.

Against

1 There are many doctors who question the positive effects of cannabis for medical use. Medical opinion has always been split. No real trials have been thoroughly carried out.

2 Cannabis smoking leads to increased cigarette smoking. This costs the country millions of pounds and thousands of needless deaths. We should be encouraging an active healthy lifestyle, not drug dependency.

3 Some studies have shown that cannabis users become more lazy and lethargic, lacking enthusiasm and drive. Is this what we really want young people to be like?

4 Amsterdam has become a mecca for drug dealers and dope-heads from all over the world. Do we want these people in our backyard?

5 There have been over 100 drug deaths in Strathclyde alone. How can we be sure that once cannabis is legalised, young people may not want stronger buzzes?

6 While the law is often not enforced, at least the fact that is illegal stops some people from risking their health. Do we really want to join a campaign to encourage people to pickle their brains? Are there not more important issues to campaign about?

ACKNOWLEDGEMENTS

The illustrations were drawn by Hardlines Illustration and Design.

The publishers would like to thank the following for permission to reproduce copyright material: BBC Scotland, The Guardian, The Herald and Evening Times newspapers, Scotland on Sunday, The Scotsman. Every effort has been made to trace ownership of copyright. The publishers will be happy to make arrangements with any copyright holder it has not been possible to contact.

The publishers would like to thank the following individuals and institutions and companies for permission to reproduce photographs in this book. Every effort has been made to trace ownership of copyright. The publishers will be happy to make arrangements with any copyright holder whom it has not been possible to contact:
ActionPlus 5(top); Fiona Edwards 14 (bottom); Fiona Nicholson 10 (bottom); Glasgow City Planning Department 57 (top two); The Herald, Glasgow 26, 27; Mirror Syndicate 31, 38, 108, 121; Newsroom Scotland 117; News Team International, Birmingham 29; Nora Radcliffe MSP 21(top right); PA Photos 14(top), 21(top middle), 32 (all three), 33, 46, 57 (bottom), 66, 68, 75, 85 (both), 87, 98; The Scotsman 4, 21(top left), 21(middle left), 60; Spindrift 61

The authors would like to thank the following individuals and organisations for their assistance:

Dougie McKenzie, Alec Morris, Dave Dempster, Ian Bell, Michael Horne, Aisha Ullah, Jeremy Klayman, Michael Ford, Omar Rana, Gary McIntyre of Boroughmuir HS
Bronwen MacKay, Moira Scott, John Russell at BBC Scotland
Alasdair McKee, Glenoaks Housing Association
Shenaz Bahadur, Equalities Unit, City of Edinburgh Council
Stephen Fitzpatrick, Scottish Local Government Information Unit
Fife Council Social Work Service
Parveen Khan, Equal Opportunties Commission, Glasgow
Scottish Executive Children and Young People's Group
Andy Kerr MSP
John Barnes
Lis, Mary and Joe McTaggart
Frank and Betty Petrie
Joe and Kate Duffy
Stephen Halder, Charlotte Litt, Julia Morris and Elisabeth Tribe at Hodder & Stoughton Educational.

John McTaggart, Principal Teacher of Modern Studies, Boroughmuir High
Allan Grieve, Assistant Head Teacher, Falkirk High

Orders: please contact Bookpoint Ltd, Milton Park, Abingdon, Oxon OX14 4SB. Telephone: (44) 01235 827720. Fax: (44) 01235 400454. Lines are open from 9.00 – 6.00, Monday to Saturday, with a 24 hour message answering service. You can also order through our website www.hodderheadline.co.uk.

A catalogue record for this title is available from The British Library

ISBN 0 340 77986 1

Published by Hodder Gibson, 2a Christe Street, Paisley PA1 1NB. Tel: 0141 848 1609;
Fax: 0141 889 6315; email: hoddergibson@hodder.co.uk

Published by Hodder & Stoughton Educational Scotland.
First published 2000
Impression number   10 9 8 7 6 5 4 3
Year   2006 2005 2004 2003
Cover photo from Network Photographers Ltd, London
Typeset by Fakenham Phottypesetting Limited
Printed in Great Britain for Hodder Gibson, 2a Christie Street, Paisley, PA1 1NB, Scotland, UK by The Bath Press, Bath